AMAZING FACTS: AN EXEMPLARY CHRISTIAN: GERMAN CHANCELLOR ANGELA MERKEL WHAT MAKES YOU *NOT* A CHRISTIAN

The new gospel revelations series 4

Festus Enumah M.D.

The New Gospel Revelations Series of the New Christianity of Christ *Essentials*
Made Easy
The Words and Works of Jesus Christ Decoded
Amazing Facts: An Exemplary Christian: German Chancellor Angela Merkel.
What Makes You *Not* a Christian
New Gospel Revelations Series 4
United States Library of Congress Catalog Card: TXu 2-005-841, 2016
Copyright © 2016 Festus Enumah M.D.
For information regarding permission, write to:
Festus Enumah, M.D.
1629 10th Avenue. Columbus. GA 31901. USA
The Library of Congress of United States in Cataloging
Festus Enumah M.D
1629 10th Avenue. Columbus, Georgia, 31901. USA
ISBN: 0692792120
ISBN 13: 9780692792124
Library of Congress Control Number: 2016917060
Festus Enumah, Columbus, GA

DEDICATION

This book is dedicated to:
Millions of refugees worldwide and to those who are helping them.

Other books by Festus Enumah M.D.

The Innocent Blood and Judas Iscariot

The Father's Business and the Spiritual Cross

The New *Gospel* Revelations Series 1–The Naked Truth: Jesus's Kingdom of God and its Mysteries decoded

New *Gospel* Revelations Series 2-Easter Decoded: Jesus's Everlasting Miracle of the Earthly Stages of Human Creation

The New *Gospel* Revelations Series 3-Game Over: ABC's of Eternal Life and Jesus's Role in Human Creation.

Coming soon.

The New *Gospel* Revelations Series 5-The Mysteries of Golgotha: Why Jesus Died

Volume 1 New Christianity of Christ Essentials Made Easy.

The Words and Works of Jesus Christ Decoded

(The New *Gospel* Revelations Series 1-1V)

ABOUT THE BOOK COVER

Front Cover
The spiritual events in Jerusalem and at Golgotha carried all the divine portraits of the events at Golgotha, where Jesus was crucified and placed them conspicuously in the human consciousness for everlasting remembrance. Jesus's words of compassion, love, mercy, humility, and forgiveness were the epitome of His earthly lifestyle. In medicine, compassion, empathy, humility, love for the sick and dedication manifest profoundly beyond the boundaries of ethical and moral professionalism in the practice of medicine. It is for these reasons that the book cover was designed, bearing with it, the Oath of Hippocrates, shaped in the form of a cross.

The image is from a 12ᵗʰ century Byzantine manuscript. Vatican Bibloteca Apostolica, Rome.

Back Cover
The back cover of the book portrays the footprints of the twelve ordained apostles, whose feet Jesus washed during the Last Supper in preparation for their travel to the Greco-Roman Empire and to all parts of the world, in order to spread the good news of Eternal life, what it is, why we need it, how to obtain it and to educate and reveal to the public what they observed and learned from Him on how to be a Christian.

I imagine that a few hundred years hence, there will be found to exist in the intellectual ideas which we shall have left behind us much that is contradictory; people will wonder how we put up with it. They will find much hard and dry husk in what we took for the kernel; they will be unable to understand how we could be so shortsighted and fail to get a sound grasp of what was essential and separate it from the rest. Someday, the knife will be applied and the pieces will be cutaway where as yet we do not feel the slightest inclination to distinguish. Let us hope that then we may find fair judges, who will measure our ideas, not by what we have unwittingly taken over from tradition and are neither able nor called upon to correct, but by what was born of our own, by the changes and improvements which we have effected in what was handed down to us or was commonly prevalent in our day.

Adolf von Harnack
What Is Christianity. P.55
1986 Edition

The thief cometh not, but for to steal, and to kill, and to destroy: I am come that they might have life, and that they might have it more abundantly.

—Jesus. John 10:10

TABLE OF CONTENTS

INTRODUCTION

But seek ye first the kingdom of God, and his righteousness; and all these things shall be added unto you.

—Jesus. Matthew 6:33

The words and works of Christ are the foundations upon which the Christian religion is built. They are centered on Jesus Kingdom of God and the eternal life that resides in that Kingdom. This spiritual life is what is in the Father and Jesus Christ, endowed to human souls through Christ and to all who are willing to receive it. To have this spiritual life now and continue to have it after death is what makes you a Christian. The most important thing in Christianity is Jesus's Kingdom of God and not the events at Golgotha where Jesus was crucified. The cross was positioned along the trajectory Jesus used to reveal the deep mysteries of His Kingdom of God and its infinite power in human creation. Jesus's Kingdom of God is His religion. The Gospel of Jesus Christ is the Gospel of His Kingdom of God. It is the Gospel of what makes you a Christian. It was delivered to us in words as the Sermon on the Mount. (Matthew 5-7) A synopsis of it was prescribed and dispensed to us as the Lord's Prayer.(Matthew 6:9-13; Luke 11:2-4) It was demonstrated to us by Jesus's earthly lifestyle and by His everlasting miracle of the earthly stages of human creation. How to be a Christian and what to do when you become one, was revealed in many of Jesus's words on eternal life and in many parables of the Kingdom of God. Why you need to be a Christian was demonstrated by His epic miracle of the earthly stages of human creation. Jesus used Himself as a model, demonstrating in essence the prototype of a Christian!

If you want to be called a Christian, you must enter into that Kingdom of God, experience it and manifest the features of the nature of the Father in that kingdom to the world by your words and works. Eternal life is the life in the Spirit of the Father, given to us as a gift through Christ. We need it to be participants in our earthly stages of human creation, as proclaimed, prescribed and demonstrated by Christ in His miracle of life. In the transcendental transformation of the human soul in its creative evolution as it seeks to be fully created, the human soul needs to achieve that goal: life of the Spirit of Christ in the created spiritual being. As the human soul with eternal life positions itself in the human creative trajectory, it is powered by Jesus's Kingdom of God. Eternal life, a gift from the Father, given to all human souls through Christ, positioned itself on the trajectory of all the earthly stages of the human creative process and continues to be the dominant spiritual life after resurrection for those who inherited it before death. To be a Christian you must enter into Jesus's Kingdom of God to possess this eternal life. To be in Christ is to possess this life of His Father that is in Him. Jesus came to give us the same life in Him as in the Father.

Jesus's Kingdom of God also revealed the nature of His Father that is a component of that Kingdom. To be a Christian you must be a partaker of the nature of His Father by manifesting the features of the nature of the Father as proclaimed by Christ and demonstrated by His earthly lifestyle. Jesus went to many cities and villages revealing the nature of His Father. The epitome of the earthly life of Jesus is the mirror through which we see all these reflections of the nature of the Father. Manifesting the feature of the nature of the Father in that Kingdom is more than the moral and ethical experiences practiced before Christ came. In this 21st century the epic human experience of it, was precisely demonstrated by the German Chancellor Angela Merkel in her dealing with the migrant refugees. What Jesus did for mankind opened a vast spiritual kingdom of His Father in human souls. Our task, if we are willing, is to open our hearts to the incoming iridescent heavenly rays from the glorified Holy Ghost (the Spirit of the risen Christ) to rekindle and activate the latent power and life of that Spirit of the Father in our souls, given to us through Christ. That was precisely what Chancellor Angela Merkel and the German people that supported her did. Their experience provided evidence that what happened to the apostles two thousand years ago on the day of Pentecost, is still happening today. The German people did not speak in tongues as the apostle did after they had received the Spirit of the risen Christ. They spoke with tears in their eyes, with money, food and clothing for the refugees. They spoke with compassion, mercy and love that extended to people that they never met in their lives. They knew that they are Muslims and yet they spoke in the language all the refugees understood by opening the German boarders and admitting them into their country. The *modus operandi* of the manifestation of Jesus's Kingdom of God within their hearts was an exemplary exhibition of the working formulation of the 21st century Christians. "God, who commanded the light to shine out of darkness, hath shined in our hearts, to give the light of the knowledge of the glory of God in the face of Jesus Christ." (2 Corinthians 4:6) It was the light that illuminated their hearts.

During His earthly life, Jesus enjoyed an enviable unbroken bondage and experience with this God, His Father: "As the living Father had sent me, and I live by the Father." (John 6:57) Despite all the obstacles Jesus encountered in the execution of the will of His Father, He continued to believe in Him. His infinite love for mankind remained unchanged as was demonstrated by His lifestyle. It was a lifestyle of labor of love, that expounded the moral and ethical doctrines practiced before He came into an infinite, untouchable experience of what is in the nature of His Father: love that extended to the enemy, the just and the unjust, the good and the bad; mercy and compassion to the unknown.

The sporadic terrorist attacks in Germany could not stop the manifestations of that love. Chancellor Angela Merkel was very sympathetic to the families of the victims of the attack. However, she said after the attack that she will not change the refugee policy. What is hidden behind their actions is the indescribable, untouchable divine light they have inherited in Jesus's Kingdom of God and manifested to the world. It was the same heavenly light in the nature of the Spirit of the Father in Christ that Jesus manifested in many of His actions and prescribed such actions for us. What they executed was the defining moment in history, never seen since the period of crucible Christianity, when the earthly phase of eternal life-the life of the Spirit of the Father in human souls given to us through Christ-manifested in great measures. It expressed itself in the pursuit of a great mission, extending love to the unknown, safeguarding that love and guaranteeing the perpetual continuity and safety of that love to all who seek that love of the Father regardless of their religious background. Chancellor Angela Merkel and the German people became the vehicle for the manifestation of that divine love of the Father and Jesus Christ to the world.

If we have to understand the Christianity that Jesus proclaimed, prescribed and demonstrated two thousand years ago, and comprehend what makes us a Christian or not, we must first understand His Kingdom of God, the eternal life within it, His nature, the Father who sent Him and the objectives and goals of that His Kingdom. The exemplary action of Chancellor Angela Merkel and the German people revealed to the world, the indestructible spiritual thread that originated from the Father and connected all mankind. This invisible thread is Jesus's Kingdom of God within their souls that they activated to achieve the objectives and goals of that Kingdom, revealing in essence, that common thread that unites all mankind. They had entered into that Kingdom, inherited the life of the Spirit of the Father (eternal life) bestowed to them through Christ, became partakers of the nature of that Father, manifested their infinite experience of that nature of the Father that is outside the spectrum of moral and ethical doctrines practiced before Christ came. They are the ones that have inherited eternal life by the purity of their hearts and as partakers in the nature of the Father, have positioned themselves in the earthly stages of the human creative trajectory to be fully created as demonstrated by Jesus in His epic miracle of human creation.

CHAPTER 1
AN EXEMPLARY CHRISTIAN: GERMAN CHANCELLOR ANGELA MERKEL

By viewing the refugees as victims to be rescued rather than invaders to be repelled … the pastor's daughter wielded mercy like a weapon. For asking more of her country than most politicians would dare, for standing firm against tyranny as well as expedience and for providing steadfast moral leadership in a world where it is in short supply, Angela Merkel is TIME"s Person of the Year 2015.

—TIME Magazine December 21, 2015

We feel the misery of each individual refugee. Humans have a responsibility to help.

—Dalai Lama. June. 2016

Wir schaffen das. (We can do this)

—The German Chancellor Angela Merkel 2015

Give ye them to eat.

—Jesus. Mark 6:37

**Come, ye blessed of my Father, inherit the kingdom
prepared for you from the foundation of the world: for
I was hungry, and ye gave me meat: I was thirsty, and
ye gave me drink: I was a stranger, and ye took me in:
naked, and ye clothed me: I was sick, and ye visited me:
I was in prison, and ye came unto me. Then shall the
righteous answer him, saying, Lord, when saw we thee
hungry and fed thee? Or thirsty, and gave thee drink?
When saw we thee as a stranger, and took thee in? Or
naked, and clothed thee? Or when saw we thee sick, or
in prison, and came unto thee? And the King shall answer and say unto them, Verily I say unto you, Inasmuch
as ye have done it unto one of the least of these my breth-
ren, ye have done it unto me.** *Then shall he say also unto
them on the left hand, Depart from me, ye cursed, into
everlasting fire, prepared for the devil and his angels: or I
was hungry and ye gave me no meat. I was thirsty, and ye
gave me no drink: I was a stranger, and ye took me not in:
naked, and ye clothed me not: sick, and in prison, and ye
visited me not. Then shall they also answer him, saying,
Lord, when saw we thee hungry, or athirst, or a stranger,
or naked, or sick, or in prison, and did not minister unto
thee? Then shall he answer them, saying, verily I say unto
you, Inasmuch as ye did it not to one of the least of these,
ye did it not to me. And these shall go away into everlasting punishment: but the righteous into life eternal.*

—Jesus. Matthew 25: 31-46

The story of the German Chancellor Angela Merkel with the migrant refugees is the greatest story since the time of Saint Paul. It is the story of a happy ending to the fiery tale of human suffering. For a long time now, I have been on the watch, looking for the fourteenth apostle of Christ. I explored Butlers' lives of Saints and found none. I surveyed the past and the present history of the Popes, the Archbishops of Canterbury, Nobel Peace Prize Winners, and the past and present world leaders and world religious leaders and found none. Then something dramatic happened. If today, the story of Cleopas and his friends, who on their way to Emmaus, unknowingly entertained the risen Christ, was repeated, with the German Chancellor Angela Merkel as Cleopas and the German people that supported her as the companions of Cleopas, they could say today, "Did not our hearts burn within us while they were feeding and housing thousands of those migrant refugees that the risen Christ was with them" It brought to memory the many human faces of Christ and a reminder of His words: *"Inasmuch as ye did it not to one of the least of these, ye did it not to me."* It brought to our memory, the agony and the sufferings of those refugees from the bombs and ethnic executions in their countries, as they left the dead family members, relatives and friends and ran from their countries seeking shelter and protection. The amazing fact is that the majority of those refugees are Muslims. No human being has the power or authority to ordain another an apostle. If we have that authority, the German Chancellor Angela Merkel would be ordained today as the fourteenth apostle of Jesus Christ.

As the act of Mary in anointing Jesus with the costly oil before His last journey to Jerusalem, is a memorial whenever the gospel is preached; likewise, whenever the act of the German Chancellor Angela Merkel and the German people who supported her, greeted the refugees with cheers, and carried the placard "Welcome Refugees" will be a memorial whenever the new Christianity of Christ is preached. Jesus spoke of the feeding of His sheep. His instruction to Peter was this: if you love me, feed my sheep. (John 21:15-17) The Chancellor and the German people fed more than a million of Jesus's sheep. The fulfillment and the illumination, in this 21st century of what Jesus said two thousand years ago provided the proof of the divine origin of His words and the existence of the source of those words: His Father.

> *For I have not spoken of myself; but the Father which sent me, He gave me a commandment, what I should say, and what I speak.*

—Jesus. John 12:49

Since I have been exploring this new Christianity of Christ, I was not able to find anyone since the time of Paul that truly embodied all that Jesus Christ proclaimed, prescribed for us and demonstrated by His lifestyle and His epic miracle of life on what makes someone a Christian. That search ended. The quest to be like Christ, His apostles, and Paul catapults one to the past and makes such a lifestyle difficult to achieve in this age of technological and scientific advances, in a world community that treasures power and wealth above all things. The German Chancellor Angela Merkel changed everything. At last, she came forward and gave the world a practical demonstration of what Christ proclaimed, prescribed and demonstrated during His earthly life.

While the Christians are waiting for Christ to come back again, and the archaeologist, in search for Jesus, are digging up places in Palestine, Chancellor Angela Merkel and her German supporters and other members of the European Union, saw many faces of Christ in all the refugees. It was the greatest staged re-entry of Christ into our world in this century. The new Christianity of Christ reasserted itself, revealing in essence that it has been moving with all the advances of mankind but human beings failed to recognize it and move along with it.

The largest assemblage of the refugees happened in the last week of September 2015. The place was on the German borders. We all witnessed that event. Did we not? Day after day, the world was bombarded with the news of the desperate journey of the refugees from the war torn nations of Syria, Afghanistan, Lebanon, Libya, Palestine, South Sudan, Turkey, Iraq, Somalia, Ukraine, Central African Republic and Democratic Republic of Congo as they ran away, seeking asylum in foreign countries. Many of them including children, died in the process. Most of them were Syrians fleeing from the war in their country. The UNHCR reported that more than four million people fled Syria since the conflict started in 2011 and more than half of them are children. Many countries refused them entry. In Syria, for example, more than two hundred and fifty thousand people have died since the war started and more than twelve million displaced from their homes. Nobody is ignorant of the bleak future of those people as a result of the devastations that occurred and is still occurring. The world's leaders, unable to find a peaceful solution, resolved to more air strikes, making the condition more intolerable. Some of them resorted in supporting the 'rebel groups.' Those policies have done nothing but produce more refugees and prolong their agony. The truth is that none of them have had the experience of being a refugee. Round table conferences became a venue for trading barbs at each other.

German Chancellor Angela Merkel was not ignorant of what was happening. In the last few weeks of September 2015, she opened all the German borders to refugees fleeing war and misery. During that period she authorized the entry into German of eight hundred thousand refugees. That number was increased to one million. By the time this book goes into print, there will be more than 1.5 million refugees in Germany. Germany and other nations of the European Union will eventually be home to more than 7.4 million refugees and their families. She is still not blinking an eye.

When more than three thousand refugees have died, including children, the German Chancellor Angela Merkel, daughter of a Lutheran Minister, found herself at the gates leading to heaven, and with the power of Jesus's kingdom of God within her, that manifested in love that extended to people of all religious faith, compassion, humility and mercy, opened those gates to the refugees to gain entrance. Germany became earthly heaven to those refugees. This is how the epic miraculous event should be told to all our children in all parts of the world.

The German Chancellor Angela Merkel opened the door that we may see Jesus's ever changing face, hear His voice in different languages and see His companions among people of all religions that was showcased as the refugees, the poor who were thirsty and hungry, the homeless who were forced to abandon their homes because of the wars and the motherless and the fatherless children whose parents were killed. By divine selection, the apostles were ordained by Christ. The selection of the apostles for their ordination by Jesus was not by any parameters known to any human being. There was no campaign, no referral, no consultation, no election or vote. They did not come from wealthy families. They were neither the most educated nor the brightest. They were the best to do the work for Him. For the last two millennia, no one has done what the German Chancellor executed with profound humility. The migrant and the refugee crisis challenged all the principalities and Faith of all world religions and the leaders of the great nations of the world. Some nations barb-wired their borders, sprayed the refugees with tear gas. Many put up insurmountable obstacles that kept the refugees at bay. Christ knew who would do the work for Him. Her name is Angela Merkel, the German Chancellor. Her parents must have observed something special on her face when she was born that they named her Angela. Remove the last letter, what is left is Angel.

When more than a million refugees assembled at the German borders, the German Chancellor Angela Merkel did not see them as Muslims or Islamic extremist coming to invade her country. She did not see them as "one of the great Trojan horses." She behaved as if she was there at Golgotha, standing on the hillside, and watching Jesus on the cross of suffering. She knew precisely the weapon that Jesus used for victory. Love that extended to people she never met before, mercy and compassion-consistent with what Jesus prescribed in His Kingdom of God and demonstrated at Golgotha-became her weapons in dealing with the refugees. Angela is TIME's Person of the year 2015. She is more than that. The German Chancellor Angela Merkel is the fourteenth apostle of Christ that I have been searching for and the first Christian of the last two millennia. The future of the world would be in good hands if only we could find leaders like her. What does her action mean to us today? The action of Angela Merkel exemplified what the entire mankind ought to do for one another: love one another and let the tentacles of that love extend to all people of the world regardless of their ethnicity or religious beliefs.

I had the experience of misery of refugees during the Nigerian civil war that ended in early 1970. As a medical student, I was the regional Director of the Sick Bay Clinics where refugees also obtained medical care. I gained insight into the plight of refugees. Today, we are dealing with refugees from Syria, Iraq, Afghanistan, Yemen, Libya, Palestine, sub-Saharan African nations and from many other countless poor nations. The miserable conditions of those refugees are well documented in many publications. We do not know what the future holds. If we continue in our destructive trajectory, we may in future have billions of refugees from the best developed nation of the world. We may ourselves be refugees one day. How then do we deal with the problem? The best defense is to eliminate the conditions that are the root causes that lead to the production of refugees: hatred and jealousy, wars, ethnic and religious persecutions, religious extremism, human right violation, ignorance of who we are and why we are here, lack of basic knowledge of the intrinsic value of human life.

Angela Merkel gave us a practical demonstration of what to do if we are confronted with mass displacement of people that presented as refugees. Jesus's teachings on mercy, love, compassion, kindness and selfless service were given the greatest demonstration that the world had not witnessed in the last two thousand years. Chancellor Angela Merkel followed what she did by opening the German treasure house and gave billions of Euros to nations supporting the refugees. Today, she is still actively involved not only in providing protection and security to the refugees but also in crafting plans that would eliminate the root causes that produced and continues to produce the current refugee crisis. All that Christ prescribed in His New Christianity were illuminated by her action.

The world witnessed Jesus's Kingdom of God in action as was manifested by her action with the refugees. It provided proof that Jesus's Kingdom of God did not fade away. What the Chancellor Angela Merkel did was a miracle that revealed the power of Jesus's Kingdom of God within her that manifested itself in love, mercy and compassion to millions of refugees. With the command of her words, the German borders opened; the sick received medical treatment, the children got milk, food, clothing and shelter, the unaccompanied children who lost their parents were protected, the disabled got support, and many that lost members of their families from the guns, artillery and tank shells, missiles jet fighters and bombers or drowned at sea during the desperate journey as they fled the war zones, were comforted. The unmanageable problems became manageable. Unfortunately, the conditions that caused the displacement of people are still going on. Today, the continued catastrophic armed conflicts in Syria, Yemen, Iraq, Afghanistan and Democratic Republic of the Congo are the root causes for the current refugee crisis. The story of the German Chancellor with the refugees is also the story of humanitarian workers that stood on the German borders, or on the front line in the conflict zones, delivering food, medicine and clothing to the people trapped behind. Jesus's commandment to "love thy neighbor as thyself and do unto others as you would like them to do unto you," was executed by Chancellor Angela Merkel and the German people who supported her and put on the imperishable show case for the entire world to see.

Those entrusted to demonstrate the power of Jesus's Kingdom of God by manifesting their experience of it are out in the world collecting earthly treasures, seeking earthly glories and power, drinking the best wines, eating the best food, driving nice cars and using their private jets to spread the Gospel of Christ. Meanwhile, the poor, the homeless, the refugees, the sick who cannot afford payment for healthcare, the elderly and Jesus's 'sheep' are neglected and relegated in the background. Many world leaders are simply silent on the current refugee crisis. Some nations and religious organizations refused to admit any of them into their communities and viewed Angela Merkel's action as something that will precipitate the economic collapse of European Union, and will encourage the spread of Islam and along with it the Islamic extremism. Some nations and religious leaders admitted insignificant number of refugees for the camera, as a political tool. The flagship, bearing the news of what Chancellor Angela Merkel and the German people did and are still doing for the refugees docked at the ports in all our capital cities, all our villages, religious institutions and their gated communities, all the White House's of Presidents of all nations, offices and homes of all heads of world corporations, offices of all lawyers, the offices of all military institutions worldwide, and at the gates of NATO, the United Nations Commissioner for Refugees (UNHCR), WHO for refugees, IMF, World Bank and World Trade Organization. They are not ignorant of what is happening. The vital question is this: are they using the same tools-compassion, mercy, love to people that you do not know and are not from the same religion- used by the Chancellor Angela Merkel in her efforts to find the solution to the current refugee crisis? If they are using the same tools, the current refugee crisis, war in

Syria and in all conflict zones will end within twenty four hours. The current refugee crisis provided mankind with the rare opportunity to observe and learn, not only to be active participants in the support for the refugees, but also to deploy Jesus's tool of love that extended to the unknown and has been demonstrated in this 21st century by Chancellor Angela Merkel, to avoid future calamities that would produce mass refugees in all nations. The world must learn how to manage refugee problems and resolve conflicts with those tools. Any other methods will simply result in more wars and increase in the number of refugees worldwide. The consequences of our inaction could lead to a global war like the one the world never witnessed before. All who may survive will find habitation in a global refugee camp.

Who in all our imaginations, would think that a person who would do the same thing as the apostles and Paul, when confronted with the same problem, would come from Germany, the country that started the Second World War? Nevertheless, in His own city Nazareth, Jesus said to His people: "But I tell you of a truth, many widows were in Israel in the days of Elias, when the heaven was shut up three years and six months, when great famine was throughout all the land; But unto none of them was Elias (Elijah) sent, save unto Sarepta, a city of Sidon (not in Israel), unto a woman that was a widow (to sustain him). And many lepers were in Israel in the time of Eliseus (Elisha) the prophet; and none of them was cleansed, saving Naaman the Syrian." (Luke 4:25-27) Naaman was a military captain in Syria who had contacted leprosy and no one could cure him in Syria. Although before September 2015, Germany, Sweden and others have taken in thousands of refugees; the new Syrian refugee crisis that subsequently evolved was considered an insurmountable problem. The Syrian refugees by divine selection, as was in the case of Naaman, the leper, who went to Eliseus from Syria, landed on the borders of Germany, seeking safety and protection in a country under the leadership of Chancellor Angela Merkel. The refugees admitted into Germany in the month of September, 2015 did not go to America, Russia, China or United Kingdom. Only a few countries offered support to the Syrian refugees. Many of the great world religious leaders remained silent, some offered lukewarm support. The miracle that happened in Germany was witnessed by the entire world. That person who behaved like the Apostles, Paul, Elisha and performed more miracles, if you take in consideration the number of the refugees involved, is Chancellor Angela Merkel. She was supported by her own people and other members of European Union.

He that receives you receives me, and he that receives me receives Him that sent me. He that receives a prophet in the name of a prophet shall receive a prophet's reward; and he that receives a righteous man in the name of a righteous man shall receive a righteous man's reward. And whosoever shall give to drink unto one of these little ones a cup of cold water only in the name of a disciple, verily I say unto you, he shall in no wise lose his reward.

— Jesus. Matthew 10:40-42

A city that is set on a hill cannot be hid. Neither do men light a candle and put it under a bushel, but, on a candlestick; to give light unto all that in the house.

—Matt 5:14-15

There is no humanitarian response that is able to solve all the current refugee problems of today. However what the German Chancellor did and continues to do is this: she rekindled that light that was set on the hill and for the last two thousand years, mankind put it under a bushel. That light is the Spirit of Christ in human souls. In essence, by her action, Jesus's Kingdom of God was rekindled.

As mankind moves along the path we call progressive evolution in science and technology, Jesus's Kingdom of God was relegated to the back ground. Christianity of Christ, as prescribed, proclaimed and demonstrated by Christ, is pushed under the rubbles of today's religion-induced wars, torpedoed by the social media and hampered by misunderstanding of Jesus' Kingdom of God, held at ransom by the Old Testament literature. Christianity once again freed itself with what the Chancellor Angela Merkel did for the refugees with the support of those German people who supported her. Jesus's open invitation to all, to have a taste of the new wine and manifests the experience of it, still stands today. Chancellor Angela Merkel manifested the experience of Jesus's Kingdom of God by the love, mercy and compassion she bestowed on the refugees, people that she had never met before. She provided the evidence that Jesus's Kingdom of God is still active even in this 21st century. The amazing and fascinating fact is that she has not stopped in her quest to help the refugees. She has had multiple consultations with the leaders of EU and other nation on the refugee crisis and pledged financial support. Recently she visited Nizip refugee camp near the Syrian border with senior EU leaders. Undaunted in her efforts on refugees, she called for the creation of "safe zones" inside Syria to shelter the Syrian refugees. If implemented and expanded this could end the Syrian war. With the support of United States and Russia, financed by China and Japan and Saudi Arabia, that would not only provide safe haven for the refugees but enhance the cessation of all hostilities. But for political and financial gains, what Chancellor Angela Merkel proposed was opposed by nations and organizations who do not want the war in Syria to end. It is my belief that the leaders of three great nations-United States of America, Russia and China-could end the war in Syria in one week, not by force, but unselfish negotiation for peace and cessation of all hostilities. What Chancellor Angela Merkel and her German compatriots did, as they opened up their home and country to more than 1.5 million refugees in a moment of time, was a demonstration that the invitational door of the new Christianity of Christ to enter into Jesus's Kingdom of God, is still open as was portrayed in the parable of wedding invitation. It was an open invitation to share the gift of the Spirit of God, the Father of Christ, with all mankind regardless of the religious beliefs. It was an invitation to the refugees to share the glory and the blessings bestowed on the people of Germany. It was an offer to all refugees, if they are willing, to share the glory of the cross and participate in Jesus's wedding feast. The big question is this: What will Jesus Christ and His Father do for Chancellor Angela Merkel, the German people and other members of the European people that supported her? I leave that question for the reader to answer.

If you want to know if you got the Sprit of Christ, look at the Chancellor Angela Merkel and her German supporters. If you want to know if you are a Christian, look at her and follow her to the refugee camps. If you are not a Christian and want an experience that will convince you to be one then follow her to the refugee camps and see the results of man's inhumanity to mankind. If you want to know if your name is also written in heaven as Angela Merkel and her German supporters is, go again and again to the locations where the refugees are camped. Let the refugees tell you stories of their lives and goals before the war and what has become of them now. Let them show you pictures of the great devastations of their homes and properties. Let them show you the pictures of their dead children, husbands, wives, relatives and friends buried in mass graves. Allow them to tell you the stories of their desperate journeys as they ran from their homes. If you want to walk on that evolutionary earthly creative trajectory pathway, learn how to participate in Jesus's everlasting miracle of creating yourself, and then follow the footprints of this exemplary Christian of the last two millennia who walked on the foot prints of Christ and is still doing so. If you want to enter into Jesus's Kingdom of God and manifest it, then follow her, observe and learn. When her autobiography is written, historians must remember one fact: that what the German Chancellor Angela Merkel did, resurrected the entire world community that was on the brink of extinction and laid the groundwork for dialogue in conflicts-not air strikes, not wars, not ineffective ceasefire declarations-but mercy, tolerance, compassion and love for the world, not just love of self and one's own country. The ground for this love is that it is what the Father does and what Jesus died for to show us how much He loves us.

The story of Chancellor Angela Merkel is the story of the migrant refugees in their desperate journey. It is the story that puts her without-any competitor-on the front line for the next Nobel Peace Prize. It is the story of the new Christianity of Christ that is still active in the world today. It is the story that gave us proof in this 21st century that Jesus really resurrected and is still active in the world. It is the story of the manifestations of Jesus' Kingdom of God in love, mercy and compassion. It is the story that brings the reality of the story of the Good Samaritan and implanted it in our consciousness as a reminder of all that Jesus prescribed. It unfolded all the portfolio of that love of the neighbor with the ability to look beyond external appearances and religious background. It revealed what we have in common and what we need to inherit eternal life and be active participants in the earthly stages of our creation. Jesus allowed Himself to suffer, be crucified and died to demonstrate to us what is revealed in the story of the German Chancellor Angela Merkel and her people with the migrant refugees. It is the story of the exemplary Christian in the last two millennia since Paul.

Ye are the light of the world. A city that is set on a hill cannot be hid. Neither do men light a candle, and put it under a bushel, but on a candlestick; and it gives light unto all that are in the house. Let your light so shine before men, that they may see your good works, and glorify your Father which is in heaven.

—Jesus. Matthew 5:14-16

It is my hope that this light set upon the hill by the German Chancellor, will shine into the hearts of all world leaders and any-one in a leadership position, rekindling in essence, their own light within, that the world may see their lights as we see the light of Angela Merkel, and glorify the Father in heaven. May all the bless-ings of heaven be on her and on the German people and members of the European Union that supported her.

Blessed are the merciful, for they shall obtain mercy.

—Matthew 5:7

CHAPTER 2

WHAT IS THE NEW CHRISTIANITY
OF CHRIST?

The new Christianity of Christ presented in this epiphany was introduced to the world two thousand years ago, with Jesus's proclamation of the kingdom of God and His demonstration of what is human life. I still call it new on the ground that today, mankind is using less than ten percent of what was prescribed, proclaimed and demonstrated by Christ. It has as its objectives: the revelation of the Father and the demonstration of the fulfillment of that one promise of the Father to humankind-the gift of His Spirit through Christ for the completion of human creation that has been going on since the first creation of mankind. The goal of its Founder, Jesus Christ, is to teach and demonstrate to mankind how to participate in the earthly phase of that creation and to gather together, in one fold, all the created spiritual beings from this planet Earth and from the other parts of the vast Universe and present them, all in one vehicle, to His Father for inheritance of the kingdom prepared for them from the foundation of the world. "Come, ye blessed of my Father; inherit the Kingdom prepared for you from the foundation of the world." (Matthew 25:34)

It catapulted the human soul to a new era, to infinite boundless unimaginable worlds of the spirits that is at present beyond mankind's intellectual understanding.

The Christianity of Christ is a functional spirituality powered by Jesus's Kingdom of God. It opened a floodgate of heavenly light from His Father to shine into our hearts. That heavenly light is the Spirit of Christ. It enabled the human souls to inherit eternal life from the Spirit of His Father through Him. It opened the door of knowledge of His Father, who is Jesus Christ, who we are and where we are going. It enabled us to be spectators and participants of the earthly stages of our creation as demonstrated by Jesus in His epic miracle of human creation. It revealed many of the mysteries of Jesus' Kingdom of God:

The power to perform miracles
The power to speak in tongues
The creative Spirit of the Father in that Kingdom
The power of creation as demonstrated in His epic miracle of human creation
The power of resurrection
The life (eternal life) of the Spirit of His Father as divine element in that kingdom
The power to dispense the Kingdom of God to human souls.

The introduction of the Christianity to the world was the defining moment in the history of humankind, when the Father decided to reveal Himself and Jesus Christ and provided us with practical demonstration of what they have been doing-human creation-since the beginning of time by sending down Jesus to this world. It marked the epoch when the Father fulfilled His promise to continue creating us through the glorified Spirit of the risen Jesus Christ that was made manifest on the day of the Pentecost. That was the Good News of this new Christianity of Christ. Within this Christianity is the story of the developmental spiritual growth of the human soul as it progresses the earthly phase of the creative trajectory to its full expression. It grew out of the seed through the Spirit of the Father that was planted by Jesus Christ as was portrayed in the parable of the Sower. The Christianity of Christ is "the seed which a man cast into the ground, and should sleep, and rise night and day, and the seed should spring and grow up, he knows not how. For the earth brings forth fruit of herself; first the blade, then the ear, after that the full corn in the ear, but when the fruit is brought forth, immediately he puts in the sickle, because the harvest is come." (Mark 4:26-29) It is like the mustard seed, the smallest of all seed, but when planted, grows to be the biggest of all trees. Its growth is irrepressible. It will increase and expand worldwide-despite all the obstacles mounted on its trajectory, bearing with it, the robe of Christianity, the Spirit of Christ. It was for the propagation of the objectives and goals of this Christianity that on the day of the Pentecost, the promised Spirit of the Father, sent in the name of Christ as the Holy Ghost (the Spirit of the risen Christ) was bestowed on the apostles. (Acts 2:1-4)

Adolf von Harnack in his book on *What is Christianity* gave an excellent exposition on the developmental history of Christianity. He called it "an exhibition of the Christian religion in its leading phases in the Apostolic Age, in Catholicism and in Protestantism." I recommend it to anyone who seeks to have an understanding of the doctrines of today's Christian groups and how they evolved. This is outside the scope of my treatise. Many Christians are aware that there is something going on that is not right. They are afraid to talk about it. They are fearful of being labeled non-believer, a sinner, an atheist or a heretic. They are fearful that they will end up in hell if they challenge the authority of the Christian leaders. The members of the Christian communities are afraid of being excommunicated by their leaders. What is amazing about the Christianity of today is the enormous power and influence the leaders have on the people. Is this power and authority real? Perhaps they can use this influence and the vital information in this my epiphany to preach what Christ, proclaimed, prescribed and demonstrated, and use themselves as models in the execution of what we must do to make a difference in this troubled world.

At the time of Christ, the Jewish religious leaders had the same power and influence on the Jewish people. The new Christianity that I recovered in its original context is powered and sustained by Jesus's Kingdom of God. It is directed, even as of today, by Christ who was given all authority and power on earth and in heaven by His Father. It is rooted in what Jesus proclaimed, prescribed and demonstrated by His life examples and by His epic miracle of Human creation. In its portfolio, no one except Christ is given the key to the Kingdom. The implication that the apostle Peter was given the key to the Kingdom and to admit whomsoever he wanted, implies that Peter can endow the Spirit of the Father to human beings. Only Jesus Christ was given such authority from His Father. However, the author of that text was thinking of the Kingdom in heaven or the Kingdom Jesus will restore to Israel.

What the New Christianity of Christ proclaimed in its doctrines:

Jesus's kingdom of God within human souls
  Words of eternal life
  The will of the Father and the commandments of Christ
  Eternal life through Jesus's Kingdom of God
  Jesus's authority to dispense that eternal life to human souls
  God, the Father of Jesus-whom the world did not know before Jesus came-as the Creator and a true God. (John 17: 3, 4)
  Jesus Christ as also a God and a Creator
  Jesus of Nazareth as the Christ sent to this world by His Father, our God.
  Infinite Trinity of the human souls with Jesus and His Father.

The real Christian Faith, its core element, as prescribed, proclaimed by Christ before and after His resurrection is His Kingdom of God. It is the centerpiece of Jesus's Christianity and His religion. From its beginning to this moment in this 21st century, everyone, Jesus Christ, His Father and all mankind are in it. There is something holy and spiritual in it for us that was given to us as a gift by His Father through Him. It is the fountain of life or what Jesus called the living water. The new creature, evolved from that living water as was verbalized and demonstrated by Christ. In the encounter to the Samaritan woman, Jesus said to her:

> *If you know the gift of God, and who it is that said to thee, Give me to drink; you would have asked of him, and he would have given you living water....Whosoever drinks of this water shall thirst again: But whosoever drinks of the water that I shall give him shall never thirst; but the water that I shall give him shall be in him a well of water springing up into everlasting life.*

> —John 4: 10, 13, 14

This living water is metaphorically the eternal life, an essential divine element in Jesus's Kingdom of God that life originated from the Spirit of His Father. It depicted the nature of His Father

We cannot understand any form of Christianity that is out there, until we comprehend the meaning of Jesus's Kingdom of God. To comprehend its mysteries, we must first enter into that Kingdom and experience it. When this mystery is digested, and absorbed (Jesus likened it as eating His flesh and drinking His blood) what is revealed is true life with Christ, a life that will live forever. (John 6: 53-58) How to get this life and bond with the loving Father and Christ is the goal of the true Christianity. In it there is no seat for the God that Moses revealed to the Jews. There are no rooms for the doctrines of atonement or any of the seven sacraments. There is no room for Christianity, Judaism, or any other religion in it as prescribed, proclaimed and practiced today, but there are unlimited spaces for all their members and their leaders who are ready to be participants in what Jesus prescribed, proclaimed and demonstrated.

Without Jesus's Kingdom of God, there will be no Christianity that would be of any credible form. It makes the biggest demand on all of us. Our ultimate task is this: To voluntarily allow the Spirit of Christ in our hearts evolve and grow, in the earthly phase of our creation, that we may live. This is the mystery of our existence and our glorious destiny. This is our ultimate chance for our transcendental transformation of our earthly life to eternal life with Christ and His Father, designed for all mankind.

What the New Christianity of Christ prescribed are:

Enter into Jesus's Kingdom of God and manifest the experience of it with love that extends to the enemy, forgiveness, mercy, compassion avoidance of hatred and revenge, selfless service and justice. These are what that soil needs for the seed-the Spirit of the Father- that was implanted by Christ, to sprout and grow to full maturity as was portrayed in the parable of the Sower. In essence, use the Spirit of the Father given to you through Christ to participate in your own creation to full expression as a spiritual being. This is the most important thing for the human race.

Refusal to be an obstacle to His Kingdom of God. In essence do not plant 'thorns that would choke the seed.' The journey in the earthly phase of human creation is powered by Jesus's Kingdom of God. Do not be an obstacle to that process.

Participate in the preparation of the soil (the human souls) for planting of the seed by the Sower. Jesus revealed what you have to do in His sermons on the mount, in the

Lord's Prayer as to produce good fruits as listed in His Beatitudes.

Participate in all the activities of the Kingdom of God and encourage others to do so.

Complete obedience to the will of His Father. There is only one will of God for

Humanity: to believe in Jesus Christ whom He sent, (John 6: 40)

Obey Jesus's commandments. (John 14:21; 15: 10)

What the New Christianity of Christ demonstrated:

(Jesus used Himself to accomplish that task-and portrayed in the parable of the Sower)

The manifestations of the power of Jesus's Kingdom of God in miracles

Epitome of the life of Jesus Christ

The journey of the human soul in its creative trajectory to its full expression.

Jesus's staged everlasting miracle of human creation, using Himself as a model

The prototype of the created spiritual human being

What the New Christianity of Christ revealed:

The Foundation of Christian Faith is Jesus's Kingdom of God

Why Jesus allowed the Jews to condemn Him to death and offered no resistance to His crucifixion at Golgotha by the Romans.

That God, the Father of Jesus is not the same God of Moses

Jesus's demonstration of the everlasting miracle of the earthly stages of human creation t provided proofs of His role in human creation and the existence of His Father

The power of Jesus's Kingdom of God in all His works

God, the Father as the Creator and the only true God who reigns and controls all things

Who is Jesus Christ

Who we are and why we are here

The intrinsic value of human life.

The participation of mankind in the earthly stages of human creation

The destiny of resurrected human spirits in the spiritual worlds of Christ and His Father

That His Father, our God sent Jesus to this world

The mystery of the Christianity of Christ, is the mystery of this uninterrupted, imperishable human creation that is still going on now under the directorship of the Father and Jesus Christ. If we are to worship God, the Father of Jesus Christ in truth, our hearts must understand who we are worshipping. If the leaders in Christian religion are to 'bring people to Christ' they must not only understand that this Christ belongs to the Father and not to the God that was revealed by Moses to the Jews. They must also have entered into the Kingdom of God and manifest the experience of it by the examples in their lives. If the world would be a safer place for our children and for us, we must teach the children the truth of why Jesus came. If we must stop killing one another and help eliminate evil activities in the world, we must take a good survey of Christianity as prescribed and practiced today by its leaders and what is perceived as the truth by the Christians and compare them with the nature, objectives and the goals of the Christianity of Christ as to harness its glory. If we are to place the words and the works of Christ alongside the advances in science and technology and see the connection, then we should look at the Founder of this Christianity, His divine authority from His Father, what He prescribed, proclaimed and His demonstration of the earthly phase of human creation. There will be no science or

technology without Him. In essence, there will be no human being on this planet without Him and His Father. If you believe that
the Father and Christ are creating human beings, as I have been
presenting in this epistemology, then without them, you would not
have been born into this world!

The Christianity of Christ does not see color or boundaries
between nations. It sees no Chinese, no American, no African or
Indian, no Italian, no black or whites, no Native Americans or
Mexicans, no Catholics or Protestants, no Muslims or Christians,
no liberals or conservatives as enemies. It seeks to unite all as one.
It opens the heart, enabling it to explore the vast mysteries of the
Gospel, which reveals the truth and the true meaning of the kingdom of God. Christianity is a platform to be used by mankind to
liberate themselves from the shackles of evil forces hatred, racism,
greed, violence, and progresses to great moments in its spiritual
evolution. It looks for both the good and the bad, planting in their
hearts Christ's spiritual forces for the transcendental transformation in our creative process. It seeks in essence, to be the guardian
of the human soul in the journey to our celestial destiny.

If Christianity and the teachings of the Gospel are to spread to
all nations, then Christianity has no other option than to continue
the great spiritual movement of the original Christianity, planting
without violence Christ's spiritual forces in the hearts of humans
who are looking, longing, and silently working toward great moments of new experiences with the God-Jesus Christ-human spirit
association that would enable God to complete His business in creating humans in the imagery and likeness of Christ. This is in essence what the Christianity of Christ is. If Christianity is to "drink
of the cup" that Jesus drank from and be "baptized with" the baptism of peace, tolerance, suffering, sacrifice, obedience to the will
of the Father and forgiveness,(Mark 10:39) its Master was baptized
with, then Christianity has no other option than to reveal to humanity what Christ, prescribed, proclaimed and demonstrated in
Palestine. Christianity must instruct all its members to participate

actively in all of Jesus's divine instructions and commandments, or, as John the Baptist addressed it, be baptized with fire, lest we make mockery of Jesus's everlasting miracle of the earthly stages of human creation.

What started as the Christianity of Christ, sustained as the Christianity of the Apostles by the apostles, Paul and early Disciples of Christ, was changed to Christianity of Faith as practiced today. Many external elements were incorporated into it. Today, there are multiple fragmented Christian Faiths with many features of the original Christianity of Christ was lost in translation. The incorporation of external elements into all the diverse groups of Christianity has continued to the present time. It would seem that the only thing left in the Christianity of Christ is the Spirit of Christ and that other core elements vanished and need no longer be taken seriously. Despite all the obstacles mounted against it, it is still active and vibrant today. Its core divine elements are irrepressible and untouchable. The Christianity of Christ in this epiphany, took a quantum leap, bypassed all the many diverse Christian theologies and groups, pushed aside the sacraments and the human dogmas, carried all the earthly human souls in their evolutionary creative journey, to the spiritual Golgotha, revealing its glory-the glory of the resurrection of Christ and the revealed prototype of the created spiritual mankind. It bypassed the God that Moses revealed and carries with it the stamp of His Father, our God. "I have not spoken of myself, but the Father which sent me, He gave me a commandment what I should say and what I should speak." (John 12:49) What I have done in the presentation and recovery of the Christianity of Christ is to bypass all external elements incorporated in many groups of Christianity as prescribed, proclaimed and practiced today by many Christians. They all pose as obstacles to the active divine spirituality of the Christianity of Christ and would be explored later in this current epiphany. This approach validates the legitimacy-not by hope, not by human doctrines or faith as defined today-of Jesus's practical demonstrations of the objectives and goals of the Christianity that He introduced to the world. There are many works of His Father that we do not know. However, the ultimate work that the Father sent Jesus to do for mankind, resides in the depths of this Christianity,

The introduction of the Christianity of Christ marked a turning point in our history when the holy armament for the earthly phase of our evolutionary creative process was placed at our disposal. Christianity of Christ is not a religion. It is a spirituality that is found in depths of all religions of this world. As long as human beings are involved in those world religions, then the Spirit of the Father through Christ is involved. No one knows Christianity of Christ in full and will never know it as prescribed by Christ because what He revealed is only a segment of it. Many of its divine imprints are still hidden and perhaps its mysteries would be revealed when we can look again at the God, the Father that He revealed and adequately interpret Jesus's Kingdom of God, His death and resurrection. Jesus had said that "No man knoweth the Son but the Father; neither knoweth any man the Father save the Son, and he to whomsoever the Son will reveal Him." What I am reporting here is what I found by looking at what Jesus wants to share with all humankind: the Spirit and knowledge of His Father, the knowledge of His own Spirit in human souls. In essence, Jesus wants us to know Him and His Father. The Christianity of Christ revealed the love and mercy of His Father and His gift to humankind.

The Christianity of Christ carries the light that illuminates the earthly phase of the evolutionary creative pathway that our journey may not end in darkness. "I am come a light into the world, that whosoever believeth in me should not abide in darkness." (John 12:46) That light was not put under the bed but on a candle sticks that all may benefit from it. "That was the true Light, which lighteth every man that cometh to the world." (John 1:9) With this light one can easily identify potholes in life along the trajectory of our creative pathway and bypass them. The Christianity of Christ has its own intrinsic protective power. Jesus allowed the Romans to crucify Him. In doing so, as I revealed in my book *the Father's Business and the Spiritual Cross,* the human souls were protected by the destruction of the Greco-Roman Gods, liberating the souls of the people that worship them. Even as of today, Christ gave the assurance that "I am with you always." It has the power that we can harvest and use it to control hatred, wickedness, racism, hypocrisy, extreme greed and poverty. It has the medicine that nations can take to cure them of the malicious desire to exploit the poor nations. The power and medicine reside in Jesus's Kingdom of God that sustains and propels the Christianity of Christ.

Christianity of Christ is an evolutionary science whose laboratory is the Gospel Jesus introduced two thousand years ago. The real truth of that spirituality is hidden in the words and the works of Christ and not in the physical Temples or Cathedrals. Its Temples are the human souls. It seeks mercy and forgiveness for the enemy; love for His Father and for one another. It seeks no human or animal sacrifices for the Father and disengaged itself from all sacraments and human doctrines. Incorporated in the Christianity of Christ is a way of life that is in Christ. This way of life that is in Christ is the manifestation of the experiences of Jesus's Kingdom of God. Christ's Christianity is the spirituality that guides the human soul in its journey to the spiritual worlds of the Father and Jesus Christ. It is an evolutionary active divine element planted along the human creative pathway. It is for this reason that the Christianity of Christ will not disappear until the last human being is created. Christianity of Christ is the mortar that bind together the common humanity that mankind refused to acknowledge.

CHAPTER 3

THE ROBE OF CHRISTIANITY: WHAT MAKES YOU A CHRISTIAN.

*But seek first His kingdom and His righteousness and all
these things will be given to you as well.*

—Matthew 6:53

*Why do you call me Lord, Lord and do not the things I
say do?*

—Jesus

The Christianity of Christ is Jesus's Kingdom of God in action. To enter into that Kingdom is to put on the robe of Christianity. Jesus used the metaphor of the wedding garment to describe it in the parable of the wedding feast. (Matthew 22:11-14) Jesus's Kingdom of God is more important than the significance given to His death and resurrection on the ground that without the power of that Kingdom, Jesus could not have been able to resurrect Himself as to complete

His epic miracle of human creation that enhanced our understanding of human creation and the infinite power of that Kingdom. Jesus's death and resurrection were the platforms He used in the execution of the epic miracle. Jesus's Kingdom of God is the most valuable precious gift from the Father to all mankind. Jesus compared it to a treasure of esteemed value and a pearl of great price.

The kingdom of heaven is like unto treasure hid in a field; that which when a man hath found, he hideth, and for joy thereof goeth and selleth all that he hath, and buyeth that field. Again, the kingdom of heaven is like unto a merchant man, seeking goodly pearls: Who, when he had found one pearl of great price, went and sold all that he had, and bought it.

—Matthew 13: 44-46

Jesus's Kingdom of God is at the center of all His words and works. Any directives on what makes us a Christian or not, must come from the platform of that Kingdom as proclaimed, prescribed and demonstrated by Christ. All other venues are closed.

The apostles, Paul and early Christians clothed themselves with that robe and made a gallant exhibition of Jesus's Kingdom of God in action in their earthly lives. For Christianity to claim its authenticity as a true religion, those who call themselves Christians must put on the robe of the Christianity of Christ. To enter into that kingdom, inherit the eternal life in it, experience it, proclaim and practice what is prescribed by Christ for the manifestation of the experiences of that kingdom is to be clothed with the robe of Jesus's Christianity. From the moment of this experience, everything external-hatred, the quest for earthly treasures by stealing from others, hypocrisy, greed, racism, killing one another-vanishes and along with it are the followings:

The hope for the return of Christ in future to establish the New Earth and the New Heaven

The Messianic ideas about Christ
The concept that Christ died for our sins
The concept of redemption and atonement assigned to
the death of Christ

The experience of Jesus kingdom of God brings with it the experience of the life of His Father and the experience of the nature of that God that manifests in love, compassion, forgiveness for the enemy, perfection in goodness, righteousness and mercy It positioned the human soul with that experience to ascend the trajectory path of the human creative process as it strives to be that new creature that God, the Father and Jesus are creating in righteousness and true holiness. (Ephesians 4: 24) THIS IS THE EXPERIENCE THAT MAKES YOU A CHRISTIAN. Jesus Christ was sent down as a human being and demonstrated this experience by His earthly lifestyle and by His epic miracle of the earthly stages of human creation. He used Himself as a model and revealed in essence, the prototype of the first Christian!

The meaning of Jesus's kingdom of God and how to enter into it was the subject I explored in the *New Gospel Revelations Series 1 The Naked Truth: Jesus's Kingdom of God and its Mysteries Decoded.* How to inherit eternal life was also discussed in *The Gospel Revelations Series 3 ABC's of Eternal Life.* To enhance the comprehension of this section of the epiphany, it is necessary for me to list again the divine components of Jesus's Kingdom of God in human souls of those that entered into it. Jesus was given power to give the Spirit of His Father to human souls. Jesus's Kingdom of God within the human soul carries with it the following divine elements of the Spirit of His Father:

Power to perform miracles
Power to speak in tongues
Power to retain the Creative divine element (Eternal life)
Power of resurrection

Power to be partakers in the nature of the Father: love compassion, mercy, forgiveness
Protective power

I am sure that there are many essential divine elements in it that will unfold in the future. As we advance in our spiritual evolution, the mysteries will be revealed. Today we have lost the power to speak in tongues and many have lost the power to perform miracles. To create spiritual mankind and give spiritual life to what they are creating are the main objectives of that Kingdom. The experience of the full spectrum of the divine components of what is in that Kingdom endowed to human souls through Christ is what makes you a Christian. All other roads are closed. Jesus's Kingdom of God carries with it, the eternal life, and the zeal to obey the will of the Father and the commandments of Christ and to believe in them. It manifests itself in what is in the nature of the Father. The infinite power of it initiates and activates the creative element in it- the eternal life-propels and sustains the creative process of human soul that entered into that kingdom, to its glorious end.

And he said unto them, I must preach the kingdom of God to other cities also: for therefore am I sent.

—Jesus. Luke 4:43

And it came to pass afterward, that he went throughout every city and village, preaching and shewing the glad tidings of the kingdom of God: and the twelve were with Him.

—Luke 8:1

The Kingdom of God was very important to Christ. He was sent by His Father to reveal that Kingdom of God. His Father is in it. Jesus is in it. Human beings are in it if we are willing to receive it. All His words and works are connected with it. All Jesus's promises and His Father's plan for mankind are rooted in that Kingdom of God. It is the bedrock and the seed of His Christianity. All the essential elements that make you a Christian originated from it and not from the spiritual events at Golgotha where He was crucified. Jesus went to many cities and villages preaching that Kingdom of God and revealing the Kingdom's glad tidings and the nature of His Father in that Kingdom. Jesus portrayed His Father as a merciful God: "Be therefore merciful as your Father is also merciful." (Luke 6:36) He depicted God as a perfect Spirit: "God is a Spirit and those that worship Him must worship Him in spirit and in truth." (John 4:25) "The God in heaven is perfect." (Matthew 5:48) Jesus introduced a divine Father who sees in secret and knows everything we do. "But when you give alms, let not your left hand know what you right have done. That your alms may be in secret: and thy Father who sees in secret shall reward you openly." (Matthew 6:3–4) He characterized God as a good Father who loves all humankind. Jesus said to young man that called Him Good Master that, "there is none that is good but one, that is God." (Mark 10:18) The Father which is in heaven, makes His sun to rise on the evil and on the good, and sends rain on the just and on the unjust." (Matthew 5:45) "God is kind even to the unthankful as to the evil." (Luke 6:35) Jesus described the Father that forgives: "If you forgive men their trespasses, the heavenly Father will also forgive you: But if you forgive not men of their trespasses, neither will your Father forgive your trespasses." (Matthew 6:14–15) The finest illustration of the loving and the compassionate Father was portrayed in His story of the Prodigal son. (Luke 15:11-24)

The epitome of the earthly life of Jesus is the mirror through which we see all these reflections of the nature of the Father. During His earthly life, Jesus enjoyed an enviable unbroken bondage and experience with this God, His Father: "As the living Father had sent me, and I live by the Father." (John 6:57)

I always do things that please Him.

—Jesus, John 8:2

Manifestations of what is in the nature of the Father revealed by Christ and exemplified by His earthly lifestyle, is the mirror through which we are assured that those who have entered into Jesus's Kingdom of God have inherited eternal life. Those that have entered into the Kingdom have put on the proper robe of Christ and positioned their souls on the creative trajectory to be fully created in the image of the resurrected Christ. Behind the earthly lives of those people, there is something so personal, so divine and luminous, that they are indeed the light to the world and the salt of the earth. Their love extends to people they do not know and to the enemy. They leave their gift at the altar to reconcile first with their brother. (Matthew 5:23) When they judge, their judgment is true. When they give the last penny that they have, they do so with a smile, mimicking in essence, Jesus's story of the poor widow who threw two mites into the treasury as her offering. (Mark 12:-44) They are the ones that forgive more than seventy times seven. It is no longer necessary for them to speak in tongues. They speak with the power of the Kingdom of God that manifested itself in the earthly lifestyle of Christ

Because Christ also suffered for you, leaving you an example that you should follow in his steps. When He was reviled, He did not revile in return; when He suffered, he did not threaten; but He trusted to Him who judges righteously.

—1 Peter 2:21–22

Jesus did not call down fire from heaven to consume those who arrested Him. He did not call the Father to send down twelve legions

of angelic warriors to fight the Romans. He said: "Love your enemies, do good to them who hate you, bless them that curse you and
pray for them which despitefully use you and unto him that smite
you on one cheek, offer also the other and he that take away thy
cloak forbid not to take thy coat also." (Luke 6: 27–29) Jesus did
not hate those who crucified Him. Jesus prayed for them, which
was a portrayal of love and blessing for His enemies. "Father forgive them for they know not what they do." (Luke 23:36) His dis-
course on forgiveness is overwhelming. He instructed us to pray to
the Father for forgiveness: "Forgive us our trespasses as we forgive
those that trespass against us." Jesus forgave and prayed for His
enemies at Golgotha. The reason is obvious: His infinite love for
humanity. He who told us to love our enemies and forgive people
when they sin against us must do the same. If Jesus is crucified
seventy times seven, He too must forgive those that crucified Him
seventy times seven. It was what the Father would like Him to do,
it was what He wanted to do, and it was what God would like us to
do. To forgive one another is to love one another.

When the activities of those people who have put on the robe
of Christ are viewed with the periscope of Jesus's Kingdom of God,
the nature of a true Christian is revealed. The question is this: will
they continue to maintain that privilege to the end of their earthly
lives? Will they, at a stage in their creative journey, be like those
Jesus portrayed in the parable of the Sower, who did not complete
the journey because of the cares of the world, lust of other things
and the deceitfulness of riches.(Mark 4:19) Will they survive the
temptations of this world as Jesus did? (Luke 4:1-13) Are they like
the man who built his house without a foundation instead of building it on a foundation of rock? (Luke 6:48-49) In 1975, I was admitted into the General Surgery Residency program. Soon after that,
the Administrator of the hospital called me into his office. What
I thought was an invitation to congratulate me, was indeed a step
by step guide on how to stay in the program. To continue to put

on the robe of Christ, Jesus invited all to come to Him and learn how He did it.

And Jesus said unto him, No man, having put his hand to the plough, and looking back, is fit for the kingdom of God.

—Luke 9:62

Despite all the obstacles Jesus encountered in the execution of the will of His Father, He continued to believe in Him. His infinite love for mankind remained unchanged as demonstrated by His life-style. This lifestyle was of labor of love, that expounded the moral and ethical doctrines practiced before He came into an infinite, untouchable experience of what is in the nature of His Father: love that extended to the enemy, the just and the unjust, the good and the bad; mercy and compassion to the unknown.

The apostles, Paul and early Christians clothed themselves with that robe and made a gallant exhibition of Jesus's Kingdom of God in action in their earthly lives. For Christianity to claim its authenticity as a true religion, those who call themselves Christians must put on the robe of the Christianity of Christ. To proclaim and practice what was proclaimed, prescribed and demonstrated by Christ for the manifestation of the experiences and the growth of His kingdom to maturity, is to be clothed with the robe of Jesus's Christianity. All human beings received the Spirit of the Father through Christ. Mankind has no control who receives it. The gift is freely given without precondition to everyone. However, what you do with Jesus's Kingdom of God within depends on the individual as portrayed in the parable of the Sower. The same message was delivered in the parable of the Talents. (Matthew 25: 14-30)

To put on the robe of the Christ is partnership with Jesus Christ, as the human soul moves along the narrow pathway to its destination. The seed that God planted in our souls through Christ sprouted and has grown. It must grow and bloom into an image in the likeness of what was revealed on Easter. God is creating man in His own image. Jesus gave us an unprecedented demonstration of the earthly phase of that process in His epic miracle of human creation. Christianity of today was given that opportunity to direct mankind to that narrow pathway, but it failed to provide that guidance and leadership that would bring all mankind together. Instead, it became an organization that turned the worship of the Father in spirit and in truth into worship of that God in sacraments. It brought division, enslavement among its members, and definitely refused to do what Christ prescribes in His new Christianity. It engaged itself in the accumulation of earthly treasures and abandoned its leadership position as the servant of mankind. We must put on the robe of the Christianity of Christ, collaborate with Him as to harvest what His Father had planted. "Behold, I say unto you, Lift up your eyes, and look on the fields, for they are white already to harvest. And he that reapeth receiveth wages, and gathereth fruit unto life eternal; that both he that soweth and he that reapeth may rejoice together." (John 4:35-36)

What does it profit a man if he gains the whole world and loses his soul?

—Jesus. Mark 8:36

All human beings in the entire Universe, dead or living, are spiritually connected in a manner today, as was in the past. What connects us as one human community is Jesus's Kingdom of God. We cannot fully comprehend this fact at this level of our evolutionary development. What to do and how to enter into the Kingdom of God, inherit the eternal life was prescribed by Christ and demonstrated by His earthly life style. Why you need to enter into that Kingdom was demonstrated by His epic miracle of the earthly stages of human creation. To be clothed with the robe of Christ is the goal of all true Christians who want the experience of Jesus's kingdom of God. To have that experience is to be a participant in the life giving event that is happening now and will continue until the appointed time. To be clothed with the robe of Christ is to gain knowledge of His Father and Jesus Christ. It is an invisible robe that is everywhere, empowered by the Spirit of Christ. Be sure you have that garment on you before leaving this planet.

Jesus's teaching on love supersedes and overrides all moral and ethical codes that were in practice before He came. He banded together all of them in one package and called it 'love.' Jesus revealed the nature of that love by examples of His earthly lifestyle and with the ultimate demonstration of it at Golgotha where He was crucified. Jesus's commandment of love for the neighbor and for one another-the trade mark of His religion-was put on public display in Germany. It is what is in the Father's will. It is what Christ does. It was precisely what Chancellor Angela Merkel and the German people did with the refugees. To love thy neighbor is to love Christ. To love Christ is to love His Father.

> *He that hath my commandments, and keeps them, he it is that loves me: and he that loves me shall be loved of my Father, and I will love him, and will manifest myself to him.*
>
> —John 14:21

What they executed was the defining moment since the period of crucible Christianity, when the earthly phase of eternal life-the life of the Spirit of the Father in human souls given to us through Christ-manifested in great measures. It expressed itself in the pursuit of a great mission, extending love to the unknown, safeguarding that love and guaranteeing the perpetual continuity and safety of that love to all who seek for that love regardless of their religious background. Like Paul, there was no barrier to that love.

*Who shall separate us from the love of Christ? Shall tribulation, or
distress, or persecution, or famine, or nakedness, or peril, or sword?
As it is written, for thy sake we are killed all the day long; we are
accounted as sheep for the slaughter. Nay, in all these things we
are more than conquerors through him that loved us. For I am per-
suaded, that neither death, nor life, nor angels, nor principalities,
nor powers, nor things present, nor things to come, nor height, nor
depth, nor any other creature, shall be able to separate us from the
love of God, which is in Christ Jesus our Lord.*

—Romans 8:35-39

They had entered into that Kingdom, inherited the life of the
Spirit of the Father (eternal life) bestowed to them through Christ,
became partakers of the nature of that Father, manifested their
infinite experience of that nature of the Father that is outside the
spectrum of moral and ethical doctrines practiced before Christ
came. They are the ones that have inherited eternal life by the
purity of their hearts and as partakers in the nature of the Father,
have positioned themselves in the earthly stages of the human creative trajectory to be fully created as demonstrated by Jesus in His
epic miracle of human creation.

*Not everyone that saith unto me, Lord, Lord, shall enter into the
kingdom of heaven; but he that doeth the will of my Father which
is in heaven.*

—Matthew 7:21

The will of His Father is for us to believe in Jesus Christ. To believe
in Jesus Christ is simply to activate and experience His Kingdom of
God within us. The life of the Spirit of the Father in that Kingdom
is the life Jesus came to give us and give it to us abundantly. Please
do not wait after death to receive that gift. It is the light of the

hidden Paradise of His Kingdom in our souls. It is the light of the life of the Spirit of the Father in your soul, illuminating the evolutionary trajectory pathways of creation. To move along in this earthly life is like using your canoe without paddles you will be at the mercy of the currents. The waves are real. To die without activating the Kingdom of God within, is not to be born at all. In essence, if you have not entered into Jesus's Kingdom of God and manifest your experience of it, you are not a Christian.

There is a latent power of Jesus's kingdom of God in every human being which may be recognized as the passion to do good and not evil. However, this passion is dependent on good knowledge of the divine elements of that Kingdom and on the objectives and goals of the Kingdom. The world cannot move forward without that knowledge. We have always been at crossroads. We have always turned to the wrong direction that led to fear of our neighbors, fear of nuclear attack, killing of one another, inquisition that is still going on, accumulation of wealth at the expense of the poor, plunder and pillage of other nations, lawlessness, suicide, kidnapping, depression and intellectual confusion on our spirituality. Many political leaders on this planet know that to kill is not the best way to settle conflicts. Why is the practice of ordering the killing of people of other nations, sometimes their own people a common practice? Many leaders of all religions, obsessed with power and accumulating earthly treasures and money, use the religious illiteracy of their members to exploit them. The solutions to these problems are not found inside Cathedrals and Temples.

The world is again at a crossroad. Some people are trying to redirect us in the right direction. However, the majority are still moving in the wrong direction that raises the disturbing question as to the destiny of mankind. This is the time to march in the right direction. It will not be a risky journey. Yes, there may be potholes and detours along that trajectory. What we need is within us. The application of the knowledge of Jesus's Kingdom of God within us will contribute immensely. To Jesus, it is the only solution as all other roads are closed. The world has missed millions of real geniuses by refusing to educate the poor. After the last World War, the Japanese offered free education up to university level. Today, they are reaping the benefits of that policy. United States of America did not have such policy. Africa neglected education and as a result, development is stagnant. My aim in writing this epiphany is to educate the public on what Christ proclaimed, prescribed and demonstrated in a simple way everyone can understand. To use that knowledge is to enter into His Kingdom of God, inherit eternal life and manifest that experience to the world now, as you strive for full expression of that life that is in the Spirit of the Father and Jesus Christ. This is the hallmark of Christianity. This eternal life continues after death. It is a gift from The Father to all mankind through Christ to all who are willing to receive. To have the knowledge of that eternal life is to have the knowledge of Jesus's Kingdom of God that connects all mankind as one community and who we are. Application of that knowledge will redirect mankind in the right direction. All killings and evil activities will cease.

To be clothed with the robe of Christianity is to gain knowledge of Jesus Christ His Father. It is my hope that one day what has been handed down to us today by the Christian leaders and Christian theologians on what makes us Christians will vanish from human memories and be replaced with the everlasting memory of the experiences of Jesus Kingdom of God in human hearts. Jesus's appeal to follow Him is an invitation to come to Him, learn and observe how to put on that robe of Christianity, live and die with His Spirit. Be sure you have that garment on you before leaving this planet. This is what makes you a Christian.

CHAPTER 4
WHAT MAKES YOU *NOT* A CHRISTIAN

Not everyone that said unto me, Lord, Lord, shall enter into the kingdom of heaven; but he that doeth the will of my Father which is in heaven.

—Matthew 7:21

Many are called, but few are chosen.

—Matthew 22:14

Why do you call me Lord, Lord and do not the things I say?

—Jesus

Recently, in February 2016, Pope Francis responded to Donald Trump's plan to build a wall along the US-Mexican border by saying that: "This man is not Christian if he has said things like that." Donald Trump, the Republican front-runner in the campaign for United States Presidency, replied that: "I am a Christian, and I am proud of it." The public identification or our perception of a person as non-Christian may contribute to what makes us not a Christian on the ground that the person may change at any moments exemplified by the life of Paul and human beings cannot judge one another on spiritual matters. There are many ways to look at the problem.

First, we need to review again what I explored in the last chapter on what makes one a Christian. Second, we can look again at the words and works of Christ and re-explore what is the new Christianity of Christ as I have presented in this treatise. How Christianity as prescribed, proclaimed and demonstrated today, was able to transform itself, starting from the end if its crucible period to its present form, in such a way that hides the truth of the new Christianity of Christ that Christ proclaimed, prescribed and demonstrated, is beyond my imagination. Jesus precisely prescribed what makes anyone a Christian and demonstrated it by His lifestyle. His parable of the sheep and the goat (Matthew 25: 31-46) gives us an insight on what makes one His disciple or not a Christian. It became obvious that wearing the physical cross around your neck does not make one a Christian. Pinning a cross to the clothes of a priest does not make that individual a Christian. There is more to true priesthood than the cross in his or her possession. It is something spiritual that fills his or her heart with a sacred duty to love and serve God and all humanity, manifesting in essence, Jesus's Kingdom of God. True priesthood must reflect the knowledge of all the divine laws of the Father and commandments of Christ and the willingness not only to obey them with perfect obedience but also to teach mankind the ways to God, our Father. It must reflect the priest's deep knowledge of Jesus's Kingdom of God and his or her experience of it. The priest's lifestyle must epitomize his instruction to the congregation: an imitation of the life of Christ and the apostles. That is a responsibility from which Christ and His Father do not release the priest. If a priest is a blind guide to the Christian community, seeking earthly powers, accumulating treasures and became a "bind heavy burdens and grievous to be borne, and lay them on men's shoulders, but they themselves will not move them with one of their fingers" then that priest is not a Christian.

Third, we can revisit some Christian practices and beliefs to determine if indeed they are the essential necessities in the formation and sustenance of being a Christian.

The belief that the God, revealed by Moses is the same God, that Jesus revealed

The belief that the Kingdom of God proclaimed by Christ is the Messianic Kingdom

The belief that Jesus is the Christian Messiah

The belief that eternal life starts after death

The belief in the second coming of Christ (Advent)

The belief in the immaculate conception of Jesus

The belief that we are all sinners and the death of Christ wiped out our sins

The belief in the atonement death of Christ.

The belief in Trinity

Participation in any of the sacraments, including baptism and Eucharist

Praying with the Rosary or with the Chaplets

Confession of sins before a Priest

"For I have not spoken of myself; but the Father which sent me, He gave me a commandment, what I should say, and what I should speak."

—(John 12:49)

The word which you hear is not mine, but the Father's which sent me.

—Jesus. John 14:24

The words of God, the Father gave us through Jesus Christ are not found in the Old Testament texts. When the entire Christian beliefs and practices as listed above are viewed with the lens of the words and the works of Christ, they are nonessential requirements to the process of being a Christian. Some may even be considered as obstacles. They do not make you a Christian

Fourth, we can look again at Jesus's two great commandments, the Lord's Prayer and the will of His Father. They all carry the essential elements that makes one a Christian. The Lord's Prayer is not just a simple prayer, but the platform Jesus used to encrypt how to enter into His Kingdom of God, inherit what makes us Christians and manifest that experience to the world. Incorporated into that prayer is the only precondition for inheritance of the divine elements in that Kingdom: FORGIVENESS. Jesus replaced the entire Ten Commandments of Moses with His two great Commandments and graced it with the introduction of what Himself and His Father knows best: love that manifests itself with forgiveness, mercy and not sacrifices, compassion and justice. Although Jesus's two great Commandments penetrate the frontiers of the Ten Commandments of Moses, they surpass them and became what His Father wills and what He and His Father do for us and for our neighbor's sake. The two Commandments became colossal responsibilities for us from Christ and His Father. To believe in the Father and Jesus Christ is to enter into Jesus's Kingdom of God and manifest those two great commandments. To engage in activities outside the precepts of Jesus's two great Commandments, makes you not a Christian. God, our Father and Jesus Christ are prepared to wait, and do not want us to come to them without our willingness to love one another. To manifest the divine love, the same thing that the Father and Christ would do, is to be partakers in the nature of the Father.

A new commandment I give unto you, that you love one another; as I have loved you, that ye also love one another. By this shall all men know that ye are my disciples, if ye have loved one to another.

—Jesus. John 13:34-35

Fifth, if, we do not know who Jesus and the Father are, then we are worshipping other Spirits. The greatest conspiracy by the Jewish authorities against the unknown new God that Jesus introduced to them started immediately when they realized what Jesus did. They could not erase what Jesus introduced but they succeeded in Judaizing Christianity. The effect of that conspiracy persists even as of today. Christianity of today stands defenseless and powerless as many Christians worship the God of Moses and God, the Father of Christ as the same God. Many Christians still embrace the God of Moses as the Creator of the world. They use the Old Testament as the book of revelation of Jesus Christ and His Father. Marcion (182-188) who based his exploration on Paul's letters was the first to point out that the two Gods are not the same. What I recovered from the words and works of Christ points to His Father as a God no one has known before He came to this world as the Creator of mankind and the Universe. It provided evidence that Jesus is a God and also a Creator. Jesus is not the Son of the God revealed to the Jews by Moses. The first law in the Ten Commandments of Moses given to him by their God is this: I am the Lord thy God and thou shall not have other gods before me. Jesus broke that law by the introduction of a new God. He was branded a Blasphemer by the Jews who condemned Him to death and handed Him over to the Romans to be crucified. The goal of Christianity is eternal life and this is the will of Jesus Christ: "He that hears my words and believes in Him that sent me will have eternal life, and shall not come to condemnation, but is passed from death unto life." (John 5:24) If you then worship the God of Moses and not God, the Father that sent Jesus to this world, then you are not a Christian. Jesus Christ and His Father are not revealed in the Old Testament. The Old Testament is a good book of wisdom with classic poetry and the history of the Jewish people and their religion. It has nothing to do with what Christ, proclaimed, prescribed and demonstrated.

Sixth, what initiates us into the fellowship of being Christians and sustains us through that transcendental transformation to the glorious destiny of the Christian soul, is the power of Jesus's Kingdom of God and not the belief that the death of Christ brought salvation. All the works and words of Christ are rooted in the power of that Kingdom of God and on the inheritance of the divine elements in that Kingdom. It is the invisible spiritual link that connects us with God, our Father and with one another. It carries with it all the divine attributes of Christ and His Father. By vehicle only known to Christ, He transported them into the human souls. The inheritance of this Spirit of the Father through Christ to all who are willing to receive it enables us to inherit the life in the Spirit of the Father and have the same nature as Christ. "Now if any man has not the Spirit of Christ, he is none of His." (Romans 8:9b) The possession of the Spirit of Christ and manifesting it by worshipping His Father in spirit and in truth and by imitating Jesus's earthly life style is to be a Christian. If you do not possess functional Spirit of Christ, then you are not a Christian.

Seventh, we have to look again at Jesus's everlasting miracle of the earthly stages of human creation. Participation in it is essential as to be a Christian. If you have not entered into Jesus's Kingdom of God, inherited the eternal life, then you are not a participant in the earthly stages of your own creation, as I have outlined in the exploration of the Jesus's Miracle of life. All it means is that you do not possess the life in the Spirit of the Father that is in Christ. It is for this reason that you are not a Christian. The answers to the question of who is a Christian and what makes us not a Christian are portrayed in many parables and timeless stories of Christ in the Gospel.

Eighth, it is important to know that if you do not find yourself in any of the precepts that initiates and sustain someone to be a Christian that you can still be a Christian if you learn what makes one a Christian as proclaimed, prescribed for us and demonstrated by Christ, and put it into action.

Ninth, we have to look at what is happening in the world today as to gain from the new precepts of what makes us a Christian and what makes us not a Christian. Perhaps that would give us insight to the verbal encounter of Pope Frances with the billionaire Donald Trump. Many people call themselves Christians without knowing anything about Christianity. The only information they have on it is that Jesus Christ was crucified on the cross, rose from the dead on the third day and that His birthday is celebrated on the 25th of December. Many cannot even recite the Lord's Prayer. Many that can recite it are unaware that it carries with it, words of eternal life and the invitation from Christ to enter into His Kingdom of God. Some never heard the stories of the Prodigal son, the Good Samaritan or that of the rich man and Lazarus, the beggar. If one is born into a Christian family, the child becomes a Christian after baptism and the practice of confirmation supposedly seals the fate as member of Christian community. If you are born in a country where everyone is a Christian, then you become a Christian. Many Christians, as they grow up and ventured to gain knowledge of Christianity are confronted with the unexplained Christian Faith that founded itself on the Old Testament and on the God of Moses. It grounded in "Jesus was born of virgin Mary.", "Jesus died for our sins." (Romans 6:10), "Christ suffered for our sins." (1 Peter 3:18), "We are sanctified through the offering of the body of Christ once for all." (Hebrews 10:10), Jesus rose from the dead and now sits on the right hand of God," "Jesus is the Christian Messiah and we look forward for His return" and "Christ redeemed us from the Devil, the enemy of mankind." The Christians of today consider themselves as redeemed and chosen people, reconciled to God through the redemptive death of Jesus Christ. Jesus is presented today as the Redeemer and the Savior of mankind without any explanation. If you refuse to accept Jesus as such, then you are branded as an unbeliever whose final destiny is hell. The doctrine of atonement, the concept of eradication of sins by the death of Christ, the doctrine of incarnation of Jesus, the concept of Trinity and Advents are obstacles to the understanding of what makes us Christians.

The open Christian communities of the Apostolic Age are now gated communities that would not open their doors to the poor and the migrant refugees. The Vatican City opened its door to twelve refugees! All the Christian communities that house the heads of all Christian sects are all gated communities and have the same policy of discrimination against members of other Christian faiths. Many Christians and their leaders, as they wait for the second coming of Christ, like many people in the rest of the world, are insensitive to the cries of human suffering. Since the period of crucible Christianity, the re-introduction of a God that is not the Father of Christ, led Christians through the trajectory of "kill the enemy," Inquisition, Crusades and centuries of Christian directed wars. Mankind is in a nuclear Age, spear headed by two predominantly Christian nations-the United States of America and Russia-who want to control the world by their powers. Christianity has positioned itself again to repeat the mistakes of the past. That is precisely what is happening today. The most atrocious evil in the history of humans, slavery, were executed under the watchful eyes of Christianity and most Christians were participants. Most of them that participated called themselves Christians. Many world leaders watching what is happening in Syria, Palestine, Iraq, Afghanistan, Libya, Yemen and the horrifying events of the migrant refugees are Christians. They have adopted the policy of silence with one notable exemption: the German Chancellor Angela Merkel, the German people that supported her and some EU member nations. Surprisingly, China, with a minority of its population Christian, is actively engaged in providing support to the current migrant refugees.

What is happening today that has produced more than sixty millions refugees is under the watchful eyes of the two of the most powerful Christian leaders of the world. They have the power to take in all the world refugees into their countries, house them permanently and stop the Syrian war and other wars. As of today, there are more than five million Palestinian refugees. Many of them were born in those camps and some have died in refugee camps. They were not allowed to get out and see other parts of the world. Today, as I am writing this epiphany, it was reported that a Syrian is killed in Syria every twenty five minutes and one wounded every thirteen minutes. How can we call ourselves Christians if we remain silent on these atrocities? How can we call ourselves Christians if we remain indifferent to the world's homeless crisis and endemic poverty that have entrapped billions of people? The hard lesions of the past histories of solving problems with war are clear. The problems of today cannot be won by war. We have directed all our efforts in accumulating earthly treasures, retributive judgments, and evil activities directed against the people we hate. The problems of today cannot be solved by hatred.

The world stands today, on the stage of humanitarian crisis that was never seen before. We also stand at the golden age of spiritual evolution. Christianity as prescribed, proclaimed and demonstrated today is controlled by forces against which reason can do nothing. Perhaps there is constant movement within it for this to remain so. These efforts would eventually fail because human beings are getting smarter. We can assert our leadership role as prescribed by Christ or we can just sit down, and let it happen. Perhaps we are too busy to care. The pretense concern for the refugees and the problems of the poor by Christians for publicity will not work this time. What The German Chancellor Angela Merkel started can be duplicated in all corners of the world. We do not have to wait for financial support from the twenty one families who have more money than the rest of the people in the world for financial support. Angela Merkel did not wait for them. We do not have to wait for Christ to come back to teach us again how to be merciful and love one another. Angela Merkel saw the many faces of Christ among those refugees. What we need is within us. It is precisely what the German Chancellor Angela Merkel used, an imitation of Jesus's Kingdom of God in action. The refusal to use the spiritual tool that she used for the benefit of the refugees is what makes us not Christians.

When what was prescribed, proclaimed and demonstrated by the Christianity of today is completely dissected and explored, it became obvious that Jesus was right that: "Many are called but few are chosen." (Matthew 22:14) In essence, by the epitome of our lives as we have demonstrated to the world today, many of us are not Christians. God, the Father of Christ was forgotten, replaced with the subtle adaptation of the God of Moses and the Old Testament texts. Jesus's kingdom of God was relegated to the background. The fact that the Holy Spirit is the glorified Spirit of the risen Christ was hidden. The human spirit that participated in Jesus's staged everlasting miracle of human creation was forgotten. The Christians abandoned their post and their task for mankind and joined the world's treasure hunters. Church services became so traditionalized in dogmas and sacraments that we as Christians also, "for the sake of traditions, make void the word of God." (Matthew 15:6) What Christ prescribed, proclaimed, and demonstrated, that makes us Christians became an entity that time forgot. The most important thing is this: at the end of our earthly lives, are we the ones (the good Christians) that planted good trees that produced good fruits or are we the human race that planted bad tree (those who are not Christians) that produced bad fruits? (Matthew 17:16-19)

Wherefore by their fruits we shall know them.

—Jesus

Rumination: What Makes You Not a Christian

Refusal to enter into Jesus's Kingdom of God
Refusal to inherit eternal life
Refusal to manifest the experience of that Kingdom after you have entered into it
The belief that God revealed by Moses is the same as the Father revealed by Christ

The belief that God, the Father, is not the Creator

The belief that the God of Israel is the Creator as recorded by Moses

Refusal to believe in the Father, revealed by Christ

Refusal to accept what Jesus proclaimed prescribed and demonstrated by His life style and His epic miracle of the earthly stages of the human creation.

Refusal to put into action Jesus's Kingdom of God within you.

Refusal to believe in Jesus's power to spiritualize human souls with His Spirit

Refusal to believe in Jesus Christ. To refuse to believe in Christ is refusal to have a taste of His Kingdom of God.

The belief that the blood of Jesus that was shed at Golgotha wiped out your sins

If you seek vengeance and your heart is filled with hatred.

Your inability to forgive

Rely on the Old Testament texts to interpret Jesus's words and works. "All that came before me are thieves and robbers; but the sheep did not hear them. The thief cometh not, but to steal, to kill, and to destroy." (Jesus. John 10:8, 10)

Preach Jesus's Kingdom of God and refused to have a taste of it.

Refusal for others to enter into Jesus's Kingdom of God

Our current way of Christian living precludes anyone to believe that Christianity is a true religion. If all Christians live like the apostles, Paul, the disciples in the Apostolic Age and German Chancellor Angela Merkel in this 21st century, the whole world would be filled up with Christians. People of the world may call us Christians. The naked truth is that many of us are not Christians. Many Christians that had the real taste of Jesus's Kingdom of God that came with power died during the crucible period of Christianity. Since that period, the world had witness the activities of many Christians but not in large numbers. Today we still observe sporadic miracles. But the Christians are incapable of performing many of them, as they have lost that power. The world has witnessed the emergence of many 'Christians.' As of today there are more than two billion such Christians. Some people accepted the open invitation to the wedding feast but there are still many who are not wearing the proper wedding gown. Only recently, the plight of the migrant refugees, rekindled Jesus's Kingdom of God in the hearts of many people in the European Union, led by the German Chancellor, Angela Merkel, and I am proud to call them true Christians.

There is a thread of Jesus's new Christianity that is hidden in the current Christianity that must be recovered as to liberate Christianity and set us free. This thread carries with it all the divine elements in Jesus's Kingdom of God as was originally delivered by Christ. If we can pierce the veil that hides the truth, look at it with the lens of that Kingdom, then use all the vital information to do our duty to mankind and to the Father, our God, Christianity would bear many good fruits. For the sake of the Father and Christ and for humanity, we must remove from our consciousness and disregard the concept that Jesus came to this world to advance what Moses started and reveal more things on the God of Israel. It is a responsibility from which Christ and His Father will not release us. The ground for this responsibility for Christians is rooted in what Jesus prescribed, proclaimed and demonstrated in the staged everlasting miracle of human creation that revealed His Father as the only true God who sent Him from heaven that; "whosoever believes in Him should not perish, but have eternal life." The unwillingness to bear the responsibility of what Christ prescribed as I have presented in this treatise, simply makes you not a Christian.

What is important today is how we could use the information presented in this treatise to deal with what is happening to mankind. Will the Christians and their leaders abandon the current

Christian Faith and embrace the new Christian Faith that is rooted in Jesus's kingdom of God? Will they have the courage to stop the proclamation that Jesus's death was atonement and that all mankind, including children are sinners? Will they be prepared to abandon the slogan that Christianity is the only true religion and concentrate their effort on living their lives like Christ and the apostles, Paul and German Chancellor Angela Merkel? In the attempt to interpret why Jesus died, will they be able to stand up and refuse to use references from the Old Testament? Will they completely embrace God, the Father of Jesus as our God and not the God that was revealed to the Jews by Moses? Are the Christian leaders ready to reveal what is going on behind the veils of confession, sacraments, and Dogmas and abandon those practices? Will the Christians and their leaders, some of whom are heads of most powerful nations in the world today, be prepared to show to the world, by practical demonstration, that the era of wars, injustice,, taking advantage of the poor, racism, plunder and pillage of other nations, insensitivity to human suffering is over?

"It is not enough to talk about peace. One must believe in it.
And it is not enough to believe in it. One must work at it."

Former First Lady Eleanor Roosevelt

"He who joyfully marches to music in rank and file has already earned my contempt. He has been given a large brain by mistake, since for him the spinal cord would suffice. This disgrace to civilization should be done away with at once. Heroism at command, senseless brutality, deplorable love-of-country stance, how violently I hate all these, how despicable and ignoble war is; I would rather be torn to shreds than be a part of so base an action! It is my conviction that killing under the cloak of war is nothing but an act of murder."

Albert Einstein

53

*Beware of false prophets, which come to you in sheep's clothing,
but inwardly they are ravening wolves. Ye shall know them by their
fruits. Do men gather grapes of thorns, or figs of thistles? Even so
every good tree bringeth forth good fruit; but a corrupt tree bringeth
forth evil fruit. A good tree cannot bring forth evil fruit; neither can
a corrupt tree bring forth good fruit. Every tree that bringeth not
forth good fruit is hewn down, and cast into the fire. Wherefore by
their fruits ye shall know them,*

—Matthew 7:15-20

If Christianity over the last two millennia produced many good fruits, I would not have written this epiphany. I hope this platform, what makes us not Christians, will provide solutions to some of the world's problems. Will it change anything? Is it important today and in future, to know if we are not Christians? There are billions of people in this world, who are not Christians. What difference will it make to them that they are not Christians? In this my epiphany, I have provided evidence that the Game is over for the search for the Gods who are creating human beings and the exploration for the source and dispenser of eternal life is over. My hope is this: that one day, it may take another two thousand years, if we have not completely destroyed ourselves, that the entire mankind, Christians and non-Christians, will recognize the common thread that unites all human communities and take action for unity under the Gods creating them. This common thread that unites Human beings is Jesus's Kingdom of God. It is already implanted in all human souls waiting to be kindled and put into action. It is not an eschatological vision. It is a reality that would encourage us to strive to be good Christians. Many people who call themselves Christians are powerful political and religious leaders of today. Many of them think that they are Christians, but many of them are not. What makes them Christians or not Christians will determine the fate of our planet and mankind. It is of vital importance for survival that allows mankind to live in peace or be destroyed by the activation of the destructive power, nuclear chemical and biologic weaponries already embedded all around us. We are in the Nuclear Age. It is real.

What is most important in human life was demonstrated by Christ in His epic miracle of the stages of human creation. We are given the gift to be participants in those earthly stages of our own creation. We are designed to be partakers I the nature of the Father, to be perfect as Him. These are amazing blessings for all mankind. It is for these blessing and for us to concentrate on our colossal tasks as to be participants in the earthly phase of human creation, Jesus, precisely called for that abandonment of the pursuit for earthly powers and treasures, to sell our earthly possessions, distribute the proceeds to the poor, then follow Him to observe, and learn how to participate in our creation and be partakers in the nature of His Father.

In this 21st century, to add to the list of what makes us not Christians, we have to look at what is happening now as prescribed, proclaimed and practiced by today's Christianity. Many of them attract people's attention, give them hope that they are Christians, but in reality they are obstacles to what was prescribed and proclaimed and demonstrated by Christ.

> *Ye judge after the flesh; I judge no man. And yet, if I judge my judgment is true; for I am not alone* (in that judgment) *but I and the Father that sent me.*

> —Jesus. John 8:15-16

However, nobody should give up a shred of hope on being a Christian. It is never too late to enter into Jesus's Kingdom of God, and manifest its experience for your ultimate glory. A good example of it is Paul and the thief crucified on Jesus's right hand. Jesus's invitation is still open. Do not allow anyone to stop you from wearing the real wedding garment (the robe of Jesus's Christianity).

Ye are the salt of the earth: but if the salt has lost his savour, where-with shall it be salted? It is thenceforth good for nothing, but to be cast out, and to be trodden under foot of men. Ye are the light of the world. A city that is set on a hill cannot be hid. Neither do men light a candle, and put it under a bushel, but on a candlestick; nor does it give light unto all that are in the house. Let your light so shine before men, that they may see your good works, and glorify your Father which is in heaven.

—Matthew 5:13-16

The epiphany on what makes us not Christians is not an exploration with the intent to ridicule the Christians and their leaders. Its intent is to use that knowledge as tools that would put us on the right trajectory for the accomplishment of our task to ourselves, our fellow human beings, to the Father and to Christ. It would be an opportunity to put on the proper wedding gown and not to be thrown out of the wedding party as was portrayed in the parable of the wedding feast. It would empower us to seek the truth on what Jesus, prescribed, proclaimed and demonstrated. Today, as was in the past, Jesus's call remains the same; "Come, all things are ready."

I am still trying to be a Christian. Many people are trying to do so. We must not forget that many people, who call themselves Christians but are not, may in future become true Christians. Likewise, some who are today's true Christians may in future, because of the "care of this world and the deceitfulness of riches" put on the wrong wedding gown and reject Jesus's Kingdom of God. I am the biggest benefactor of what I recovered from the Gospel presented in this treatise. I am using that knowledge to know what is important in this life and what is not. It is my responsibility to share that vital knowledge with everyone. What is important now is not if you are not a Christian or if you think you are. The most important thing is to allow Jesus to resurrect in your heart, enter into His Kingdom and participate in your own creation by manifesting your experience of that Kingdom. Do not be afraid to enter to know what is behind Jesus Kingdom of God. Be a participant in the preparation for the glory that awaits all human souls. This is our greatest blessing. This is why we are here. The epiphany on: 'What makes you not a Christian,' is my attempt to get everyone on this planet to put on the robe of Christianity as designed by Christ and get into the field for the harvest.

> *Behold, I say unto you, lift up your eyes, and look on the fields; for they are white already to harvest. And he that reaps receives wages, and gathers fruit unto life eternal: that both he that sows and he that reaps may rejoice together. And herein is that saying true, one sows, and another reaps. I sent you to reap that whereon you bestowed no labor: other men labored, and you have entered into their labors.*

—Jesus. John 4:35-38

Jesus left imprints on how to be a Christian, not engraved in stones or as foot prints on the sand, but in the hearts of human beings. The German Chancellor Angela Merkel and the German people that supported her are such examples. Follow them, observe and learn how to be a Christian. What they did was an exemplary manifestation of their experiences of Jesus's Kingdom of God in action. They are the ones who harvested and collected the promised gift of the Father, the Spirit of the glorified risen Christ that was made manifest on the day of the Pentecost. They are the ones that have put on the proper wedding garments and are ready for Jesus's global banquet. This is the exemplary role of a Christian to the Father and Jesus Christ and to mankind.

Jesus has not given up hope on anyone. He came to heal the sick. The sickness is not disease but human lack of lack of knowledge of His kingdom of God, His Father, who we are, why we are here and the intrinsic value of human life. To encourage those that are not Christians to seek this knowledge, Jesus's greatest advice and encouragement to them are

> *Seek not ye what ye shall eat, or what ye shall drink, neither be ye of doubtful mind. For all these things do the nations of the world seek after: and your Father knoweth that ye have need of these things. But rather seek ye the kingdom of God; and all these things shall be added unto you. Fear not, little flock; for it is your Father's good pleasure to give you the kingdom. Sell that ye have, and give alms; provide yourselves bags which wax not old, a treasure in the heavens that faileth not, where no thief approacheth, neither moth corrupteth. For where your treasure is, there will your heart be also. Let your loins be girded about, and your lights burning.*

> —Luke 12: 29-35

That treasure in heaven is the priceless treasure of Jesus's Kingdom of God in human souls of those who entered into that Kingdom. Jesus's invitation to enter into that Kingdom is still open to everyone. Do not be left behind.

CHAPTER 5

JESUS'S PARABLES AND STORIES ON WHO IS NOT A CHRISTIAN

J esus's parables and many of His stories contain encrypted mes-
sages. Jesus fully explained the parable of the Sower because
His apostles asked Him for explanation. Those parables became
obscurum per obscurius (mystery wrapped in an enigma). It is difficult to fully understand or explain many of His stories. We have
always looked at Jesus's Parables of the Kingdom of God as portals
He used in His attempt to reveal the meaning of His Kingdom of
God and the 'glad tidings' associated with it. In many of these parables and in some of His stories, Jesus was also revealing to us the
divine mandate on how to be a Christian. Those parables and stories also contain the profiles of those who are not Christians. Jesus
used the habits of the people, their occupation and environments,
their expectations and experiences in life to depict what makes
them Christians. Retrospective analysis of the parables and stories
Jesus used touched the fundamentals of what Jesus proclaimed,
prescribed for us and demonstrated on how to be a Christian.
Those who listened to those parables and stories found themselves
in those narratives. Today, whoever you may be, regardless of your

nationality, political, religious, racial background, there are places we all fit in those parables and stories.

The fulfillment of the promised gift of the Holy Ghost (the glorified Spirit of the risen Christ) that came on the day of the Pentecost, provided proof of the divine authenticity of Jesus's words and that He came from heaven. It gave credence to His words: "And no man hath ascended up to heaven, but he that came down from heaven, even the Son of man which is in heaven." (John 3:13) The ways Jesus used some of His parables and stories to distinguish who is a Christian and who is not, revealed that He had a deeper knowledge of human activities, who we are, why we are here and our destiny before He was sent down by His Father. It gives one the impression that He was watching all our activities from heaven and continues to do so after His ascension. If you doubt this fact, read about what happened to Paul on his way to Damascus.

However, to enhance our comprehension of the parables, Jesus resorted to the use of the stories and earthly imageries that people can understand. Jesus refused to use the examples of events that happened in heaven or the imageries in heaven on the ground that people will find it difficult to interpret those parables and some of the stories.

If I have told you earthly things, and ye believe not, how shall ye believe, if I tell you of heavenly things?

—John 3:12

Today, the echoes of those parables and stories are sill heard and still have the same effect on us as they did when they were first narrated to the people in Palestine. They hold many mysteries of Jesus's words and works. When Peter asked Jesus: "Why do you speak to them in miracles?" Jesus replied: "Because it is given unto you to know the mysteries of the Kingdom of Heaven, but to them it is not." (Matthew 13:10-11) The parables and the stories explored in this epiphany are those that depicted those that are not Christians. At first when you look at those parables, you get the impression that Jesus was just revealing the way of life. However, behind that way of life is hidden what makes us not Christians and what makes us Christians. They are all linked with His Kingdom of God and not with the stories of His death and resurrection. Most of the parables started with first words: "The Kingdom of God is like" As I have persistently revealed I this epiphany, what makes us Christians is connected with human experience of Jesus's Kingdom of God. Jesus encrypted many things in His parables. What I have done in this brief outline is a prolog to one of the mysteries of Jesus's Kingdom of God: the mystery of being a Christian that Jesus encrypted in His parables of the Kingdom of God and in His timeless stories. The settings that Jesus used are good platforms that revealed:

Those who are not Christians.
What contributed in making them not Christians
The personal consequences of not being a Christian
The consequences of not being a Christian to their nations and the world
How they can change and become Christians
What happens after death to those who are not Christians
How you can be a Christian at any time in your life and still get the same reward
What would happen to our children if we as parents are not Christians

There are many things revealed on who are not Christians in those parables. I limited my report to the metaphoric labels Jesus used in the identification of those people in the parables and stories. The style I used is to maintain such names given to them as individuals or as a group and list where the parables and the stories are in the Gospels. There are many such parables and stories in the Gospels. The readers can add to the list.

The parables and stories that portrayed those who are not Christians

The Unforgiving Servant (Matthew 18:23-35). Forgiveness is the only precondition for entering into Jesus's Kingdom of God. It was one of the petitions in the Lord's Prayer. We must forgive before the Father can forgive us. (Matthew 6:14-15)

The dishonest steward (Luke 16:1-12)

The wedding feast and those not wearing wedding garments (Matthew 22:1-14)

The Great Supper and the men invited to supper and refused (Luke 14:16-24)

The Rich man and Lazarus (Luke 16:19-31)

The thieves, the Priest and the Levite in the story of the Good Samaritan (Luke 10:30-37)

The seeds that fell by the way side, on stony ground and among thorns in the parable of

the Sower and the Seed (Matthew 13:3-9; Mark 4:3-9; Luke 8:5-8)

The tree that produced bad fruits (Matthew 7: 16-20; Luke 6:43-45)

The bad fish in the fishing net (Matthew 13:47-50)

The man who built His house without a foundation (Luke 6:49)

The unfaithful Servant (Matthew 24:45-51; Luke 12:42-48)

Talents and the wicked slothful Servant (Matthew 25:14-30); Luke 19: 12-27)

The foolish Rich man and the earthly treasures (Luke 12:16-21)

The wicked Vinedressers (Matthew 21:33-41; Mark 12:1-9)

The five foolish virgins (Matthew 25:1-13)

The son who promised to work in vineyard and did not (Matthew 21:28-23)

The goat in the parable of the sheep and the goat (Matthew 25:31-46)

The Prodigal son (Luke 15:11-32)

False Prophets in Sheep's clothing (Matthew 7:15-16)

The status of not being a Christian is not something permanent. You can enter into Jesus's Kingdom at anytime in your life and still obtain all the benefits and blessings of the Kingdom as those who entered it early in their life. This was portrayed in the parable of the generous employer who paid the same to the laborers hired at different hours of the day. (Matthew 20:1-16) It is easy to enter into Jesus's Kingdom of God. If you have doubts, simply look at German Chancellor Angela Merkel and the German people that supported her in the way they handled the refugee crisis.

CHAPTER 6

UNFINISHED BUSINESS: JESUS AND THE KINGDOM OF THE DEAD

*Verily, verily, I say unto you, the hour is coming, and now
is, when the dead shall hear the voice of the Son of God:
and they that hear shall live. For as the Father hath life in
himself; so hath he given to the Son to have life in himself;
and hath given him authority to execute judgment also,
because he is the Son of man. Marvel not at this: for the
hour is coming, in the which all that are in the graves
shall hear his voice, And shall come forth; they that have
done good, unto the resurrection of life; and they that
have done evil, unto the resurrection of damnation. I can
of mine own self do nothing: as I hear, I judge: and my
judgment is just; because I seek not mine own will, but the
will of the Father which hath sent me.*

—John 5:25-30

*I am the good shepherd, and know my sheep, and am
known of mine. As the Father knoweth me, even so know I
the Father: and I lay down my life for the sheep. And other*

sheep I have, which are not of this fold: them also I must
bring, and they shall hear my voice; and there shall be one
fold, and one shepherd.

—John 10: 14-16

How the Father, our God and Jesus Christ will get people of all nations as one fold under one Shepherd (Jesus Christ) is already in place. At present, to connect all religions as one, under one true God, and see ourselves as common humanity, created equal in the sight of that God is an impassable frontier. However, let us give it time. It may take thousands of years or it may happen at any time. Our colossal task at present is to search for the truth in the religion we belong to, for the meaning of life-who we are, why we are here and where we are going-and for the liberation of human suffering. Can we, if we find the truth, have the courage to publicize it? I believe in Jesus Christ and in the Father that He revealed to the world. To put one's trust in Christ, is to ground oneself in the truth He revealed. He was sure that in the future mankind will be as one, and that everyone-dead or alive-would be given the opportunity to hear His true voice and participate in the earthly phase of human creation as was demonstrated by Christ. There is no way out. Everyone, dead or alive, will receive the Spirit of Christ. Jesus's authoritative assertion of unifying all mankind under one fold is the goal of what He proclaimed and demonstrated in Palestine. Nobody, dead or alive, will come to the Father without the experience of Jesus's kingdom of God. For Christians to claim that Christ belongs only to them is an obstacle to the grand plan of Jesus and the Father for mankind

What Jesus said about the dead, opened a floodgate that gives us insight that our planet is not the only place for Jesus and His Father's creative activities. We may be called to participate as laborers in the extra-territorial world of the spirits, to help bring our creation to its glorious end. From the utterances of Jesus on His planned visitation of the dead, it was confirmed what I have been presenting, is that death is a grand station –a mysterious platform-placed along the path of human creation. All human souls, without any exception, must pass through that grand station. As demonstrated by Jesus in His last act of the everlasting miracle of human creation, all human souls will be resurrected. What happens thereafter is very interesting. Jesus did not leave us in the dark on the fate of the resurrected souls. The apostles, Paul and those who believe in Jesus through His words and the works that He and that apostles did, will receive eternal life and go straight to Paradise and be with Him and his Father. (John 17:20-24) The thief crucified on His right hand is in the same place now. Some after resurrection will finally end up in hell as was portrayed in the story of the rich man and Lazarus, the beggar. (Luke 16:19-31) Those who never heard of what Jesus prescribed, proclaimed, and demonstrated and those who were given the wrong interpretation why Jesus came to this world would end up-after resurrection-in the Kingdom of the dead, to hear His voice and if they are willing, inherit and experience His Kingdom of God before moving forward. Even in the Kingdom of the dead, the experience of Jesus's Kingdom of God manifests itself in love, mercy, compassion, obedience to the will of the Father and to the commandments of Christ.

The extra-territorial and inter-cosmic journey of the human soul in its evolutionary trajectory is mind boggling. Our human nature at the present level of evolution limits our knowledge of the spiritual worlds. For the first time in the history of mankind, Jesus with authoritative assertion and with practical demonstrations, opened the portal of the spiritual worlds around us and may indeed also be within this planet. Jesus was in and out of this planet as a Spirit for forty days after His resurrection. During His transfiguration, the three apostles saw the spirits of Moses and Elias. By

His staged epic miracle of earthly phase of human creation and by His plan to visit the kingdom of the dead, Jesus forayed into untouched grounds that give mankind insights into the ultimate authentic vision of human life and its destiny. By doing so, Jesus established Himself not only as the Lord on this planet but also as the Lord and the giver of life to the dead, who also must have a taste of His kingdom and eat the bread of life He got from the Father as to continue the journey to eternal life. What Jesus introduced was another platform- the kingdom of the dead-where the same work of creation is going on with His Spirit. This is one of the revealed mysteries of Jesus's Kingdom of God.

This Kingdom of the dead is not a place of judgment where Jesus judges all mankind. It is not the Gahanna or a community for all the dead Christians. It is a community-in another spiritual world-of all the dead regardless of their nationality, religion, culture or ethnicity who:

Did not have knowledge of Christ and His Father
　　Never heard of Jesus's Kingdom of God
　　Were denied the opportunity to have knowledge of why Jesus came to the world
　　Did not know the meaning of Jesus's Kingdom of God
　　Died without eternal life and the Spirit of Christ
　　Heard what Christ prescribed and proclaimed, but did not understand it
　　Thought they are doing His Father's will but that was not what Christ prescribed as His Father's will
　　Attended many Church services, but the sermon concentrated more on the Old Testament texts that revealed the God of Moses as the Father of Christ
　　Were told that they are sinners and the blood of Christ that was shed on the cross wiped away their sins and they believed it and made no attempt to enter Jesus's Kingdom of God

Believed, as it was handed down to them by their Priests, that the death of Christ was an act of atonement

Believed, as they were instructed, that eternal life is only possible after death

Some resurrected souls in the kingdom of the dead may still not believe in Christ and His message. His Kingdom of God may still suffer violence. However, those that are willing to obey His commandments must inherit His Kingdom of God and manifest it in their post resurrection lives in that Kingdom of the dead. Jesus, by revealing His plan to continue His mission in the kingdom of the dead, confirmed-what we already know-the common bond of mankind: death and the common modus operandi deployed by Him and the Father for eternal life. It is reasonable to assume that Jesus would continue the same work as He did here in this world. However, everyone in that Kingdom has already passed through the grand stations of death and resurrection. Those waiting for Christ to come back may have to wait for a long time. Perhaps Jesus's planned visitation to the Kingdom of the dead is the real Advent. In essence, His coming back would not be here on this planet but in the Kingdom of the dead that many of us would inherit after death and resurrection.

Many who are destined to go to heaven may have first to go to this Kingdom to help Christ. He will need workers. So my dear readers put on your robe of Christianity and be ready. It is a team effort. Our work with Christ in the Kingdom of the dead may be on rotational bases. By His proclamation that He would go to the dead, who must also hear His voice, Jesus gave us the vital insight on what we need for the journey of the human soul to its ultimate end. As we pass through this world and other spiritual worlds, we must all hear the voice of the Lord who according to the apostle Peter "has the words of eternal life." Be sure to have this eternal life within you before your last breath on this planet, then it will not be necessary to transcend to the kingdom of the dead after resurrection. Jesus enthroned Himself as the indispensible companion in all stages of that journey of the human soul to its glorious destiny.

I am the way, the truth and the life.

—Jesus. John 14:6

CHAPTER 7

OBSTACLES TO CHRISTIANITY OF CHRIST.

"Cans't thou not minister to a mind diseas'd. Pluck from the memory, a rooted sorrow. Raze out the written troubles of the brain. And with some sweet oblivious antidote cleanse the stuff'd bosom of that perilous bosom of that which weigh upon the heart?"

Macbeth Act V 3 p. 44

The obstacles to the Christianity of Christ are so routed in our brains that we need a sweet antidote to clean what weighs heavily in our hearts. For many centuries and even in this twenty first century, what Christianity and many religions prescribed, proclaimed and practiced are so diverse and confusing that what linked mankind together as one fold, under one God is not envisioned at all. These obstacles are a serious concern for all mankind, all nations, all races, all Christians, people of other religions, all who are intellectually and spiritually awake and seek peace in this world. It is something that urgently needs our attention. There are elements of the Christianity of Christ in all current forms of Christianity and other world religions. This is the time to abandon this cloned Christianity and go back to Christ. We have to liberate the Christianity of Christ by the abandonment of the entire external human decorative elements that are choking it. We should learn how to differentiate between the old and new wine containers and the taste of old and new wines. We can discard the old clothes and put on the new robe of the Christianity of Christ. In the parable of the Prodigal son (Luke 15:11-24) the younger son who left, finally said to himself: 'no more of this way of life,' and returned to the Father. Christianity as prescribed proclaimed and practiced today, must do the same and say no more to the earthly accumulation of wealth and building of expensive Cathedrals. A churchless Christianity of Christ may be all we need in the end. What is needed in Christ's Christianity is not found in any physical building or in any earthly treasures. Christians have to say no, to the proclamation of human doctrines and dogmas, as they are not found in any of the words of Christ. They should say: no more to promoting the use of any sacraments. Christ knew that these obstacles will surface in future and called them weeds in His parable.

> *The kingdom of heaven is likened unto a man who sowed good seed in his field: But while men slept, his enemy came and sowed tares among the wheat, and went his way. But when the blade was sprung up, and brought forth fruit, then appeared the tares also. So the servants of the householder came and said unto him, Sir, didst not thou sow good seed in thy field? From whence then hath it tares? He said unto them, an enemy hath done this. The servants said unto him, Wilt thou then that we go and gather them up? But he said, Nay; lest while ye gather up the tares, ye root up also the wheat with them.*

—Matthew 13:24-29

The good seeds are the words of God, His Father, in the Gospel. The tares are the interpolations and many of the sayings that were put on the lip of Christ in the Gospel. The Christianity of Christ is not a hidden spirituality. However, to get to it, one has to pass through many obstacles mounted by mankind. This was indeed what happened since its introduction and the diverse 'faith' of many forms of Christian religions shows that it is still happening today. These obstacles are like potholes on the human creative trajectory pathway. It is not good enough to recognize and walk over them. We must repair them permanently for the generations that would come after us. Time is on the side of the Christianity of Christ. Its goals, despite all the obstacles, must be fulfilled. "Heaven and earth shall pass away; but my words shall not pass away." (Mark 13:31) It would continue to make its glory. In its irrepressible growth, as it moves along its trajectory to achieve its objectives and goals, "Every plant which my heavenly Father hath not planted, shall be rooted up." (Matthew 15:12-14) My attempt in this epiphany is not to liberate the Christianity of Christ, but an attempt to bring back what was once ours-the gift from God, the Father of Jesus Christ.

What the Christianity of Christ revealed and put in a once upon a time master demonstration-the staged evolutionary creative process of mankind-by Jesus, cannot be stopped. There can be no peace until mankind has that knowledge. Human beings will continue killing one another. Religious wars trying to reemerge now will rekindle with such intensity that will shake the very foundation of this world. We must say no to the deadly hatred of one another even among Christians. Adolf Hitler was a Christian, a son of the Church. Did he have the knowledge of the Christianity of Christ? The answer is no. Borrowing from the history of his religion, he persecuted, imprisoned in many labor camps, executed and killed what the Father and Christ were creating because of extreme hatred. Today, President Obama and President Putin are Christians and yet for political reasons they do not like one another. Do they have the knowledge of the Christianity of Christ? I believe that they do, but to 'protect' their nations, what Christ prescribed was put behind the veil for now.

We must, and we have no other option but to develop our hearts as receptive soil for the Sower, Jesus Christ as was portrayed in the parable of the Sower, to plant His seeds. We can make the soil unsuitable for planting and perish. The emergence of obstacles from the time Jesus proclaimed His Kingdom to the present time must be tackled. This is the test which requires that all mankind must all stand together. A house that is divided will fall. There is only one solution to the obstacles: eliminate all of them and reveal the knowledge why God, the Father of Jesus sent Him to the world. In eliminating the obstacles, so we must not be selective. All current forms of Christianity are on life support. To make room for what Jesus Christ started, we must take drastic actions as suggested by Christ Himself.

> *And if thy hand offend thee, cut it off: it is better for thee to enter into life maimed, than having two hands to go into hell, into the fire that never shall be quenched: Where their worm dieth not, and the fire is not quenched. And if thy foot offend thee, cut it off: it is better for thee to enter halt into life, than having two feet to be cast into hell, into the fire that never shall be quenched: Where their worm dieth not, and the fire is not quenched. And if thine eye offend thee, pluck it out: it is better for thee to enter into the kingdom of God with one eye, than having two eyes to be cast into hell fire: Where their worm dieth not, and the fire is not quenched. For every one shall be salted with fire, and every sacrifice shall be salted with salt. Salt is good: but if the salt has lost his saltness, wherewith will ye season it? Have salt in yourselves, and have peace one with another.*

> —Mark 9: 43-50

All the above are metaphoric expressions of what we have to do for full expression of whom we are. One must be ready to do whatever it takes, without danger to others, in the pursuit of this high goal. Many Christians are confused and deceived. The deception is not intentional. It came out of the entire obstacle incorporated into the Christianity of Christ. Christianity as prescribed, proclaimed and practiced today will vanish one day. It will be replaced by the true Christianity of Christ. The truth will stand out that when all the obstacles from all forms of current Christianity are removed, what will be revealed is the Christianity of Christ. Jesus used every obstacle on His path during His mission as instruments in developing and promoting His work. Perhaps what I have presented as obstacles may be instruments of growth of the spirituality Jesus introduced to the world. I am confident that what I am presenting would satisfy many who are seeking the truth of what is the Christianity of Christ

(1) Misinterpretations of Jesus's Kingdom of God

The ocean of knowledge presented to us by Christ compels us to find the true meaning of the Kingdom of God that He proclaimed. It coerces and entices us to laborers in the field with the hope that we may find that hidden treasure buried in that field. It allows us to act on our free will to sell all we have, and purchase the priceless peal of great value. It allures and inveigles us to find all the ornaments, the hidden gems in the Kingdom of God, as to participate in life and enjoy what the children who left here are enjoying with the angels. It is an illusion to think that Jesus would leave His place and glory in His Father's Kingdom to establish a Kingdom on earth and live here. When Satan during Jesus' temptation showed Him all the Kingdoms of the world in a moment of time and promised to give Him all of it, if only He would bow down and worship Him, Jesus rebuked him. During His arrest before the crucifixion Jesus made it known to everyone that His Kingdom is not of this world. "My Kingdom is not of this world" John 18: 36.

The Jews had hoped that Jesus came to establish the promised Kingdom of God on Earth as a fulfillment of the apocalyptic Kingdom envisioned by their Prophets. It did not happen. They were disappointed and concluded that Jesus was not the promised Messiah. They are still waiting for the apocalyptic Kingdom when the promised Messiah will come to establish the New Heaven and the New Earth for the chosen people of Israel. The apostles and the early Christians expected the proclaimed Kingdom of God to come during their life time. Peter had asked Jesus:"Will you at this time restore the Kingdom to Israel?" When that failed to materialize in the way they expected, they still hoped that it will come in future. They were not aware that it came already. They did not know that they performed miracles with the power of that Kingdom within them. They did not know that they were manifesting the features of what are in that Kingdom by the examples of their lifestyle. They went to many nations preaching the Kingdom of God and eternal life. They did not know that they have entered into the Kingdom of God and had inherited that life of the Father given to them by their Master. The epitome of the earthly lives of the apostles and the early Christians provided the mirror through which we can see all that Jesus proclaimed, prescribed and demonstrated on His Kingdom of God. We just could not envision that connection.

Like the apostles, the Christians of today believe in the future Kingdom of God and like the Jews are waiting for Christ who they proclaimed to be their Messiah, will to come back to establish the New Heaven and the New Earth for all people of the world. They call it Advent. The Father and Christ will reign in that Kingdom. The majority of the Christians are waiting for the new earth, when Jesus Christ will come and clean up the mess and restore His Kingdom on earth. They believe this is the place where Jesus would defeat the Devil and his demons with the twelve legions of soldiers from His Father. Jesus Christ will come from the sky and take away for the second time all the sins of the world, making everyone feel jubilant. By special invitation only, the select men and women will come from the East and West and from the North and South countries to sit at the table of the great banquet in the newly established Kingdom of God on earth. I don't know how Jesus will accomplish that, because the catholic will not sit on the same table with the Protestants; neither will the Jews sit with people from Palestine. Many Christians, if they allowed the non-Christians to participate, will insist the non-Christians have to eat of the crump from the table or wait till all of them are satisfied.

The Christians relegated Jesus's Kingdom of God to the future eschatological Messianic Kingdom that will come at the end of time when Jesus will judge the good and the evil. He will at that time destroy Satan. The difficulties encountered in the interpretations of Jesus's kingdom of God led to many misconceptions of the words and works of Christ. In essence, the realization of Jesus's Kingdom of God in our current life time was abandoned. The Kingdom of God was relegated to the background and no longer considered as the foundation of the Christian Faith. Without realizing it the Christians and their leader mounted the greatest obstacle to the words and works of Christ by the proclamation of the death and resurrection of Christ as the core foundation of the Christian Faith.

Over the last two thousand, since after the crucible period of Christianity, the light of Christianity dimmed. The light that was put on a candlestick to give light to all in the house was put back under the bushel. The salt of the earth lost its savour. The city that was set upon the hill as the Light house to guide and give spiritual direction to mankind was destroyed and replaced with Cathedrals decorated with stolen gold artifacts and treasures purchased with money from the poor. The seeds that Christ, the apostles, the early Christians planted on fertile grounds in Palestine, in Greco-Roman Empire and all over the world that had sprouted, died before they could bear fruits. The Christians were unable to manifest that light before men, that people all over the world may see our good works and glorify our Father in heaven. In this 21ˢᵗ century, that light came from the German Chancellor Angela Merkel and the German people that supported her. Jesus's Gospel of the kingdom was revamped to the Gospel of Sin, Redemption, Atonement, Salvation and Liturgy. What Jesus prescribed to us was substituted with Sacraments and Dogmas. Eternal life, the most important component in Jesus Kingdom of God was relegated to life after death.

Jesus positioned His death and resurrection along the trajectory He used in the execution of His epic miracle of the earthly stages of the human creation. The miracle, like His other miracles, was powered by the infinite power of His Kingdom of God. The relegation of Jesus's Kingdom of God to the future, led to the adaptation of the death and resurrection as the foundation of Christian piety. It ruined and impoverished Christianity and revamped it to the present form. It is my hope that the information I recovered from the true Gospel of Christ and presented in this epiphany will help us reclaim our leadership in providing spiritual guide to mankind, grasp what makes us Christians and proclaim to the world the real foundation of our Christian Faith: Jesus's Kingdom of God.

(11) Misconceptions of Salvation
A. Peter's Concept of Salvation
Peter believed in the salvation of Israel. Although he had identified Jesus as the Christ, he believed, like the other apostles that Christ is the Messiah. Jesus never verbalized that He is the Messiah. None of Jesus's words or works pointed to the type of the Messiah that the Jews were expecting. Peter wondered why Jesus did not bring that salvation promised to the people of Israel. When Peter asked Jesus, "will you at this time restore the kingdom to Israel?" he expected Jesus to say yes. But that never happened. In the early Christian movement that started with Peter, James, the brother of Jesus and

other apostles, one has to believe that Jesus is the Messiah and will come again to complete the Messianic expectations for the salvation of Israel. Peter believed that only Jesus will be mediator of that salvation. Peter did not connect the death of Jesus to the fulfillment of that promise.

After the miraculous healing of the crippled man at the temple, Peter made a bold statement on salvation: "Be it known to you all and to all the people of Israel, that by the name of Jesus Christ of Nazareth, whom ye crucified, whom God raised from the dead, even by Him, doth this man stand here before you whole. Neither is there salvation in any other; for there is none other name under heaven given among men whereby we must be saved." (Acts of the Apostles 4:10, 12) How can such a view, without any explanation on how Jesus brought salvation, find acceptance today in this modern world? How can people of other religion accept such an authoritative proclamation without any explanation? Is salvation the same as eternal life? The core message of Christ is the Kingdom of God. Is Jesus's Kingdom of God connected to salvation as proclaimed by Peter? After Jesus's resurrection Peter asked Him, "Lord, will you at this time again restore at this time the Kingdom to Israel?" (Acts 1:6) Was Peter referring to the Jewish salvation and associated Jesus as the Messiah that would make it possible? At that stage in his life, Peter knew only the salvation of Israel and did not connect the salvation to the Jesus's Kingdom of God and eternal life. The other point he referenced was a saving activity for the crippled man, that was made possible by Jesus who was crucified, died and was resurrected. The healing activity was not as a result of the death of Christ, but one that involved the saving and the restoration of the physical body of the crippled man that had nothing to do with salvation. That was consistent with the divine mercy bestowed on sick peoples by Christ. It was made possible by the healing power of Spirit of the risen Christ in Peter, bestowed on him and the other apostles. The healing power is connected with Jesus's Kingdom of God. Peter believed, like all the other apostles, in all the requirements, the religious and moral conditions outlined in Torah and the ceremonial laws that must be fulfilled by all people, Jews and Gentile converts, for the salvation of Israel. At the early age of Christianity, before the first Apostolic Council in Jerusalem about the years A.D. 46-47, they knew of only one salvation: the salvation of Israel. This is the "salvation (of the Jews) that the prophets have enquired and searched diligently" (1 Peter 1:10)

Blessed be the God and Father of our Lord Jesus Christ, which according to his abundant mercy hath begotten us again unto a lively hope by the resurrection of Jesus Christ from the dead, To an inheritance incorruptible, and undefiled, and that fadeth not away, reserved in heaven for you, who are kept by the power of God through faith unto salvation ready to be revealed in the last time. -

—1 Peter 1:3-5

Peter's eschatological salvation looked at the future when salvation would be completed on the Day of God. That day of the Lord "will come as a thief in the night; in the heavens shall pass away with a great noise, and the elements shall melt with fervent heat, the earth also and the works that are therein shall be burned up. The heavens being on fire shall be dissolved, and the elements shall melt with fervent heat. Nevertheless we, according to his promise, look for new heavens and a new earth, wherein dwelleth righteousness." (2 Peter 3:10, 12-13)

The problem here is that the apostle Peter who heard many of Jesus's words on eternal life took those words of Christ on eternal life and clothed them with the Jewish concept of salvation. Our task is to separate them. The tool that is available for this delicate dissection is Jesus's Kingdom of God.

B. The Christian concept of Salvation

This day is salvation come to this house.

—*Jesus said to Zaccheus,* Luke 19:9

The encounter of Jesus Christ with the rich man Zaccheus is the best introduction on how the Jewish writers in that one instance, tried to convince us that Jesus used the word salvation more than once. (Luke 19:1–10) Jesus told the Samaritan woman that salvation is of the Jews and made no attempt to tell her that He brought salvation to the Samaritans. Jesus's core message was the Kingdom of God and had identified Himself as one who is authorized to give that Spirit of the Father in Him-the Spirit of Christ-to human souls. The apostles and many others had received that Spirit. It is possible that what Jesus said to Zaccheus when He entered his house is this: 'the Kingdom of God-has come to you and your house hold.' This would be consistent with what Jesus went about in cities and villages preaching, giving practical demonstrations of its power in miracles and encouraging people to embrace it. That was precisely what Jesus told the sick people as He healed them: "The Kingdom of God is come nigh unto you." (Luke 10:9) Again, that was what Jesus said to the seventy men He sent out to heal the sick and preach the Kingdom of God, "Be sure of this, that the Kingdom of God is come nigh unto you." (Luke 10:11) Jesus did not send them out to preach salvation. The truth is that if we adopt the concept of salvation as defined by the Jews, it puts the objectives of our earthly life as fulfillment of all the preconditions for salvation as proclaimed and prescribed by Moses who claimed he got the divine directives from the God He revealed to the Jews. It channeled the goal of our earthly life as to be redeemed from our sins. It gave the assumption, without any proof, that we are fully created. In doing so, it became an obstacle to what Christ demonstrated in His

Miracle of the earthly stages of human creation. It points to the destiny of mankind to the eschatological and apocalyptic future Kingdom of God, when after the final judgment, Christ will gather the whole family of the redeemed for presentation to His Father. There is nothing eschatological or apocalyptic in the Kingdom of God proclaimed by Christ. It has nothing to do with redemption. Salvation of the human souls is not connected with Jesus's Kingdom of God or eternal life. Perhaps if the Christians remove the word 'salvation' from all the Christian texts, and replace it with eternal life and everlasting life-used frequently by Christ, we will see clearly and be able to interpret why the Father sent Jesus to this world. Jesus did not go to many cities and villages in Palestine, proclaiming salvation and demonstration how to obtain salvation by His lifestyle. His epic miracle of the earthly stages of human creation has nothing to do with salvation.

The central theme of the Christian concept of salvation that is presented to us is the restoration of fellowship with God-not specifying if it is the God of Moses or the Father of Jesus- by our deliverance from sins, including the original sin we inherited from Adam and Eve. They believe that the deliverance from sins was by the death of Jesus Christ. Through His death, human beings were reconciled to God through Christ, who suffered and allowed Himself to be crucified. They also maintained that the death of Jesus Christ was atonement, a ransom for our sins-a penalty Jesus paid to quell the wrath of the God who is angry with mankind. In addition, because of the death sacrifice, humans shall obtain the divine fellowship and enjoy eternal happiness and everlasting life with God and His Son, Jesus Christ. The Christians look forward to the second coming of Jesus Christ to make this salvation final at the last judgment "on the Day of the Lord" that would mark the catastrophic end of the world and the creation of new earth and new heaven. And those saved by the death of Christ will have to "wait for his Son from heaven, whom he raised from the dead, even Jesus, which delivered us from the wrath to come." (1 Thessalonians 1:10)

> *That the Lord suffered on account of sin, and in order to save men from it and that through his suffering men are actually saved from both the condemnation and the power of evil. That this salvation is immediate and certain and will be complete at last.*

Schaff-Herzog Encyclopedia of Religious Knowledge

The whole idea of salvation as perceived today by the Christians is based on the followings: that mankind by nature is a community of sinners and we inherited the sin from Adam and Eve.

All have sinned and come short of the glory of God. (Romans 3:23)
Christ died for our sins in accordance with the Scriptures. (1 Corinthians 15-3
Jesus was put to death for our trespasses. (Romans 4:25)
As descendants of Adam and Eve, we are all born in sin. (Romans 5:12)
Death is the consequence of sin. (Romans 512f)
Christ abolished death. (2 Timothy 1:10; Hebrew 2:14)
We must be saved from our sins and eternal death
Human beings are justified and redeemed by His death

The Christian concept of salvation means different things to many diverse Christian groups. Its philology and interpretations change at different periods of the history of the Church. This is well illustrated in the Roman Catholic concept of salvation when it introduced sacraments mediated by Priests to achieve full penalty of man's sin-an element they claimed is not covered by the death of Christ. Jesus had warned that that we must not sow new clothes to an old cloth or put new wine into old bottle: "No man putteth a piece of new cloth unto an old garment; for that which is put to fit it up taketh from the garment, and the rent is made worse. Neither do men put new wine into old bottle; else the bottle break and the wine runneth out, and the bottle perishes; but they put new wine into new bottles, and both are preserved." (Matthew 9:16–17) The old garment, the old wine bottle, and the old wine all represented Judaism. The new wine and the new cloth represented the truth and the Spirituality that Jesus Christ revealed. The adaptation of the Jewish salvation into what Jesus proclaimed, prescribed and demonstrated made it impossible to give meaningful interpretations of His words and work.

The intrinsic value of the death of Christ as revealed by His resurrection, becomes more comprehensible if all the laws and the ritual practices, which the Jewish people put in place to achieve their own salvation, are not considered in what Christ ascribed as saving activities. In doing so, one might gain insight into the words and the saving deeds of Jesus. The objectives and goals of His Kingdom of God do not fit well with any type of salvation as presented to us today. We must not forget that Jesus connected all His words and works with His Kingdom of God and His Father. The Jews connect the salvation of Israel to the God that Moses revealed to them. Jesus is well-versed in the Old Testament literature and in the Jewish concept of salvation. The spiritual restoration of sinners by His death to enjoy everlasting peace and fellowship with His Father was not proclaimed by Christ.

In reminiscence, the Christian concept of salvation was not original and not rooted in Jesus's Kingdom of God. It borrowed many of its features from the Jewish concept of salvation. In doing so, it associated itself with the God that Moses revealed and the Jewish apocalyptic Kingdom of God. It substituted the expected Jewish Messiah with its concept of Jesus as the Christian Messiah with the expectation that He will return to establish His Kingdom on Earth, having permanently destroyed the Devil and all his works. It lacked the divine elements and the human experience of Jesus's Kingdom of God and the eternal life within it. It excluded what was proclaimed, prescribed and demonstrated by Christ. It looked at Jesus's everlasting miracle of the human creation with only the lens of His resurrection and stumbled in its efforts to provide meaningful interpretation of that epic miracle. The tsunami effects of the Christian concept of salvation on mankind are still being felt today, that for the last two thousand years, the ship of Christianity, powered by this concept, is moving in the wrong direction. What can we do to correct it? The simple answer is this: understanding of Jesus's Kingdom of God, the eternal life linked with it, His epic miracle of human creation, recognition that God, the Father of Christ is not the same as the God revealed by Moses and our willingness to participate in the earthly phase of our creation. When he saw clearly, Paul, the champion of salvation, in his last missionary journey abandoned the concept of salvation, embraced fully and preached the Kingdom of God.

And he went into the synagogue, and spoke boldly for the space of three months, disputing and persuading the things concerning the kingdom of God.

—Acts 19:8

And now, behold, I know that ye all, among whom I have gone preaching the kingdom of God, shall see my face no more.

—Acts 20:25

Preaching the kingdom of God and teaching those things which concern the Lord Jesus Christ, with all confidence, no man forbidding him.

—Acts 28:31

We can simply do what Paul did. Again and again, we have pretended that we did not acknowledge what Jesus said: that salvation is of the Jews, let it be so. None of Jesus's doctrine originated from the Jews or from any doctrine in the Old Testament. They did not originate from the God of Moses. They all originated from His Father.

(111) The Concept of God, the Father of Jesus as the Jewish God
The editor, Arnold Toynbee, in the introduction of the book *the crucible Christianity* asked an important question:

> *"Why did Christianity and the Pharisees (i.e. modern) Judaism make their appearances in the world when and where they did? This is a historical question about events that happened some two thousand years ago. Two millennia are no more than the twinkling of an eye, of course, on the geological and, a fortiori, on the astronomical time-scale. Moreover, the question is not for academic interest. It is so clearly one of the clues to human destiny. …This is, in fact, a concern for all human beings, of all races, civilizations, and nationalities, who are intellectually and spiritually awake."*

Arnold Toynbee

The paramount question is this: are we as Christians worshipping the God that Moses revealed or the God, the Father, Christ revealed? Early in the seventh century, Prophet Mohammed introduced to the world another God-Allah. Today we still do not have the answer to Toynbee's question. The three religions that control over half the population of the world introduced their own God to the world. It is imperative that we must seek thorough understanding of these Gods. Have we not had enough wars fighting for those Gods? We fight for the world we do not understand. We fight for earthly survival in a world where no one survives. We fight for earthly treasures that we all leave behind when we die. The world is on the edge right now. Recently Pope Frances said that the world is at war. We have been at war for many centuries and still doing so today. The next world war may not be over oil, land or earthly treasures. It would be over religion and the worship of these Gods.

Since the Central African Republic declared its independence from France in 1960, it has been plagued by coups and rebellions. Despite its vast mineral resources, it is among the poorest countries in the world, its diamonds and gold plundered and pillaged by strongmen from around the world. Even before the war began, the International Crisis Group described the country as "worse than a failed state." For centuries, Muslims, Christians lived in relative peace there. Then, in 2013, a group of mostly Muslim rebels called the Seleka charged into Bangui from the north, unseating President François Bozizé. Within months, a band of mostly Christian militias, called the anti-balaka, rose up to counter the Seleka. Those fighters quickly recast their strategy as a broader crusade against Muslims, setting off a cycle of retaliatory killings that continues today. More than 450 mosques have been destroyed since the war broke out. Thousands of people have been slain, despite the presence of 10,000 U.N. peacekeepers.

However, what looks like impending disaster for mankind may indeed be the frontier of a new beginning: the quest for the truth in all religions and in the Gods that have been presented to the world. This epiphany is not on all Gods. There are many books written on that subject. The subject under consideration here is the God that Jesus revealed to the world and the God that Moses revealed to Jews.

I have throughout this epistemology, been making the point that God, the Father presented to us by Jesus is not the God that Moses presented to the Jews. Jesus proclaimed His Father as the only true God unknown to the world before He came. (John 17:3, 25) With reference to The Father that sent Him, "ye have neither heard His voice at any time nor seen His shape." (John5:37) The conception of this God that Jesus called His Father was the quantum leap that bypassed the God of Moses and all the prophetic utterances of that God of the Jews as its Spirit, through Christ, took the human souls to glory. In essence, the words of Jesus and His earthly works, took the presumed creative power away from a God-the God of Moses-handed down to the Christians as the Creator and enthroned His Father and Himself as Creators. The quest for earthly possessions-lands, bank accounts, gold, precious metals, Temples, magnificent Cathedral-are foreign to this God of Jesus, perhaps also to the God of Moses. The plan for the establishment of an earthly Kingdom on Earth: the New Heaven and the New Earth with the New Jerusalem, is not on the drawing board controlled by this God, the Father of Jesus. All religious organizations and the services that they offer to people, that are not prescribed, proclaimed and demonstrated by His Son, during His earthly mission, are of no value to Him. Many Christians will be shocked. I do not know how they will react to this great challenge. The Christian authorities may ask: how then can we preach without reference to the God of the Old Testament? How can we convince the people that this new knowledge is authentic? Do we have to rewrite all the books on creation, the sins of Adam and Eve, the doctrine of original sin and atonement? My answer is this: from the very beginning of Christianity, the Christians were constantly reminded of Jesus's sacrifice for mankind. This is our opportunity to offer our own sacrifice for Him, to love and honor Him by looking again to what He prescribed, proclaimed and demonstrated. Such a move that will bring mankind from the dump as being hostile, hostile to one another, lack of spiritual maturity, extreme geed, cut throat policies, abuse of poor nations and neglect of the poor to a higher level of spiritual evolution for maturity, unity of mankind and empowerment towards the objectives and goals of the Christianity of Christ. We can sacrifice by public proclamation of everything we know about God, the Father who sent Jesus Christ to this world and move away from the God that Moses revealed to the Jews.

The core message from the Christian leaders is God's love for mankind by sending Jesus Christ. Now it is our turn to tell Him how much we love Him by doing exactly what Jesus did as was portrayed in His prayer: "I have manifested thy name unto men. And I have declared unto them thy name and will declare it." (John 17:6, 26) Let us also declare His name and reveal it in all parts of the world. The world knew about the God that Moses revealed before Christ came, but did not know about God the Father that Jesus revealed. "O righteous Father, the world hath not known Thee, but I have known thee." (John 17:25) If you love Christ and wants to be a good Christian on active duty, on call for Jesus's Christianity, it is imperative that you too must declare His Father to the world that they may know Him as the only true God. You must, as the Preacher, in making that proclamation on God, the Father of Christ, tell the congregation, in unequivocal, absolute terms that He is not the God that Moses revealed to the world. This is your sacrifice and the way you must manifest that deep love of God, the Father that Jesus Christ revealed. This is the way to manifest Jesus's kingdom of God. It is for this love that Paul always bowed his knees unto "the Father of our Lord Jesus Christ, of whom the whole family in heaven and earth is named, That He would grant you, according to the riches of His glory, to be strengthened with might by His Spirit in the inner man; That Christ may dwell in your hearts by faith; that ye, being rooted and grounded in love, May be able to comprehend with all saints what is the breadth, and length, and depth, and height; And to know the love of Christ, which passeth knowledge, that ye might be filled with all the fullness of God." "Ephesians 3: 14-19)

(1V) Reading the Gospels with the Jewish Old Testament Lens
The Christianity of Christ is like "a red thread in the center of the web, and somewhere or other, it would emerge, afresh, and free itself from its entangling connections. Even in the outwardly decorated inwardly decaying temples of the Greek and the Roman

Church, it has not been effaced. Venture onwards! Deep down in a vault you will still find the altar and its sacred, ever-burning lamp." (*What is Christianity*, Adolf von Harnack)

With the proclamation of Jesus' Kingdom of God, the Christianity of Christ became spiritualized. As it moves along in its trajectory to achieve its objectives and goals it carries that sacred, ever-burning light, kindling the human souls, propelling it through death and resurrection to its glory. We must remove all the entangling connections—the obstacles. A major obstacle is the Old Testament literature. To find that sacred ever-burning lamp someone must have the courage to leave the Old Testament Bible to the Jews. A major change occurred along the path of the Christianity of Christ on the day the Church canonized the Old Testament literature. The mixture of the old and new wine became completed. Jesus did not explain many things to the apostles. After his departure, the apostles found the answers to some of His words and deeds, even His deed, in the Old Testament record.

> *I delivered unto you first of all, that which I alone received, how Christ died for our sins according to the Scriptures, and that He was buried, and that He rose again the third day."*

—Paul,

In another instance, it was reported that Jesus said: "Moses, write of me." If you find in the Old Testament text where Moses wrote of Christ, please let us know. The truth is this: Jesus introduced into the world something that was absolutely new. There are no prophetic utterances that pointed to Jesus or His Father.

> *I am come in my Father's name and ye receive me not; if another shall come in his own name, him ye will receive.*

—Jesus, John 5:43

Jesus was not revealed to anyone before He came. "No man knoweth who the Son is, but the Father, and who the Father is, but the Son and he to whom the Son would reveal Him" (Luke 10:22). There is not a single prophesy in the Old Testament literature that reveals Jesus' Kingdom of God or gave mankind a clue to the earthly phase of the evolutionary human creative process, initiated by Jesus and demonstrated its trajectory through His death and resurrection. In essence, Jesus' words and works have no prophetic vision. Jesus did not portray Himself as a Jewish Prophet, who usually starts their proclamations with "Thus said the Lord." Jesus stated some of His proclamations with "I say unto you." In prophesy it is believed that a God comes to the prophet and speaks through the person. Jesus spoke for Himself. Jesus's prediction of His death and resurrection or who He is was not a prophetic proclamation that was recorded in the Old Testament texts as revealed in the followings words of Christ:

> *You neither know me, nor my Father: if you have known me you should have known my Father also.*
>
> —Jesus. John 8:19

> *No man knoweth the Son, but the Father.*
>
> —Jesus Matthew 11:27

> *Blessed are your eyes, for they see; and your ears, for they hear. For verily I say unto you, that many prophets and righteous men have desired to see those things which ye see and have not seen them and to hear those things which you hear, and have not heard them".*
>
> —Matthew 13:16,17

The danger of giving prophet interpretations to the words and works of Christ is not only to associate Him with the Prophets of the Old Testament, but to associate Him with many of the eschatological and apocalyptic utterances of the Jewish Prophets that are incorporated in His Gospel. The world is still waiting for many of the Jewish prophesies to be fulfilled.

What Jesus introduced to the World-His Father, Himself, His words and His Works-were not foreshadowed in any world history or in the history of the Jewish people as recorded in the Old Testament literature. The Old Testament literature is a lethal weapon that has dragged down the Christianity of Christ to a slow pace of growth. The history of creation by the God that Moses revealed, in its early chapters put mankind on a trajectory of confusion, insecurity and fear of that God. The Christians can only do one thing to liberate themselves from the bondage: remove the Old Testament Bible as a cannon book. This may sound radical, but it is the only solution. The Jews have the right to keep that book to themselves. The Old Testament is a great book of wisdom and poetry and that is its only great contribution to mankind.

(V) The Concept that Christianity Originated from Judaism
Today, the proclamation that Christianity originated from Judaism must no longer be ignored. It is time to remove all the Jewish outer coatings that were used to decorate Jesus's robe of Christianity. If Judaism is represented as the old wine because it came before Christianity, and Christianity as the new wine, then it is time to stop mixing the old and the new wines together. This obstacle was portrayed in the parables of the old and new garments and the old and new wine bottles.

And he spoke also a parable unto them; No man putteth a piece of a new garment upon an old; if otherwise, then both the new maketh a rent, and the piece that was taken out of the new agreed not with the old. And no man putteth new wine into old bottles; else the new wine will burst the bottles, and be spilled, and the bottles shall perish. But new wine must be put into new bottles; and both are preserved. No man also having drunk old wine straightway desireth new: for he said, the old is better.

—Luke 5: 36-39

The apostles and the early Christians were Jews. They succeeded in freeing Christianity from the Jewish ceremonial laws and Temples services. However, the Torah and the Old Testaments were untouchable. To look at the person of Jesus Christ, His words and works with the Jewish lens is to look at the extraterrestrial Universe without a telescope. You see nothing. Christianity is so entrenched in Judaism for so long now, that it will take courage and sacrifice to disentangle itself from it and see what Jesus introduced to the world. It was so intertwined with Judaism that its Gospel became a fortified prison for Jesus's Kingdom of God and the Christianity of Christ. Without the knowledge of Jesus's Kingdom of God, everything that Jesus did became incomprehensible and hidden from us. The old wine was secretly poured into the new wine bottles. The Christians drank it and rejoiced. The God revealed by Moses became their God. The Ten Commandments of Moses replaced the two great commandments of Christ. They were told that during the Transfiguration, that Jesus saw "Moses and Elias who appeared in glory, and spoke of His decease which He should accomplish at Jerusalem." (Luke 9: 28-36) The Christians believed it. The Jewish Gospel stated that Jesus said that He came, not to destroy the law or the prophets, but to fulfill them. (Matthew 5: 17) The Christians believed it and could not part with the Old Testament and the Prophetic revelations on what they assumed revealed Christ, His works and His death. The truth is that Jesus Christ replaced all the moral laws in the Ten Commandments with unprecedented love for His Father and thy neighbor and replaced the first commandment with His Father as the Lord and the only true God. I have always wondered whose voice the Prophets and Moses heard, as nobody ever heard the voice of His Father.

John Shelby Spong in his book: *Liberating the Gospels* asked "How can a Jewish work be understood if none ignores the Jewish context, the Jewish mind set, the Jewish frame of reference, the Jewish vocabulary, and the Jewish history that shaped and formed the writer." It was this mind set of the Jews who narrated the works and the deeds of Christ that pose the greatest threat to the Christianity of Christ. The Jewish writers told us the story of Jesus and modified it and incorporated the doctrines of Judaism into it. The works of Christ had nothing to do with Judaism or the Jews as a special community of His Father. It was a work that looked at them as part of humankind endowed with the same gift from His Father as everyone else. There are no twelve tribes of the Jews in heaven. There are many Jews like others in heaven. The tribes as formed on this planet Earth have caused so many irreparable problems-wars, hatred, greed for lands and power-that no sensible God would think of setting up any tribal divisions ever.

All other religions have their own Gospels. Christianity of today, as it models itself to the Christianity of Christ should abandon Judaism completely and respect it as the religion of the Jewish people and not part of Christianity of Christ.

> *Difficult as it is to pour new wine into an old wineskin, this process was accomplished without great upheaval, so long as the stress level among the Jewish majority was tolerable. When that stress level reached crisis proportion however, this Christian use of the Jewish sacred material was viscerally resented*

John Shelby Spong in Liberating *the Gospel*

The Jews tried to play down, mock and distort Jesus's works and words. There is no linkage or bond between the Jewish sacred materials and what Jesus prescribed, proclaimed and demonstrated. What I would encourage the Jews to do is not just to resent the use of the Jewish sacred materials by the Christians but to ban and make it impossible for them to use them. That would mark the time in history when the light from the Spirit of Christ would eliminate all the darkness in many souls in a moment of time as we joyfully embark on our journey to our glory.

(V1) Advent (the Second Coming of Christ) and Rapture

Today many Christians are still waiting for Jesus Christ to come from heaven and establish His Kingdom on earth. Mega Churches and Temples are being built to impress Jesus when He comes back. They have completely ignored what Christ prescribed and proclaimed. The Kingdom of God even today "suffereth" violence and violent take it by force" because people have closed their hearts to Jesus' Spirit as evidenced by lack of human compassion, the torture and killings of humans, the indiscriminate use of brute force to settle conflicts and neglect of the poor and the needy. But they are eagerly waiting for Christ to return. The popular movement now among the Christians is how to get your house ready for a surprise visit from Christ when He comes back. The sad side of this anticipation is the lack of knowledge that Christ is present to this world now with many faces and "I am with you always." (Jesus. Matthew 18:20)

The Christians believe that Jesus is the Messiah whose second coming would validate His divine origin and that His earthly mission was a prelude to that grand heavenly event when He would come in glory out of the clouds. (Matthew 24:23-31; Mark 13:21-31; Luke 21:25-33) This is simply a modification of the Jewish apocalyptic concepts of their Messiah that were incorporated in the Gospel writings. To continue to believe in Advent would leave many people out in the cold, unable to participate in what Christ prescribed, proclaimed and demonstrated that is still going on now. This foolishness was portrayed by Jesus in the parable of "The wise and the foolish virgins." (Matthew25:1-13) The simple truth is that Christ is not hidden in today's world. He is not just sitting on the right hand of His Father, watching the world and waiting for the appointed time to return. Jesus Christ is here, watching everyone.

(V11) The Concept of Jesus as a Messiah
John the Baptist sent two of his disciples to ask Jesus, "Are you the One to come or do we look for another?" For hours, Jesus allowed those two men to observe His work, and then sent them back to John with this message:

> *Then Jesus answering said unto them, Go your way, and tell John what things ye have seen and heard; how that the blind see, the lame walk, the lepers are cleansed, the deaf hear, the dead are raised, to the poor the gospel is preached.*

—Luke 7:22

The Christians answered John the Baptist's question for Jesus. Based on what they had labeled 'the Messianic consciousness of Christ' the Christians proclaimed Jesus Christ as the Messiah, who would return to complete His work. Little attention was paid to the Gospel Jesus said He was preaching to the poor.

I still do not understand why Christians are not able to walk away from Judaism. Why would they not have the courage to complete what Christ and Paul started? The Messiah and the apocalyptic Son of Man concepts as portrayed in the Jewish literature were not articulated at all by Jesus yet Christ was clothed with those titles. It created the false impression that the words and the works of Christ are eschatological-apocalyptic events. It also led to the false expectation of the early Christians to hope for the immediate coming of Jesus as the Messiah to establish the Kingdom of God that He proclaimed. That hope has remained unfulfilled even as of today. The meaning of Jesus's Kingdom of God obliterated and re-directed to the wide and dangerous road that leads nowhere but to an apocalyptic Messiah who will establish the spiritual Kingdom of God as envisioned by prophet Daniel and others. The Christianity of Christ that started in a bright sunshine with the proclamation of Jesus's Kingdom of God was turned into a chilly dark environment with vague uncertainty of hope for the earthly future Kingdom and Rapture.

Jesus had no Messianic plans as being proclaimed by the Christians. His task from His Father for mankind was very specific and had nothing to do with Messianic expectations. Jesus complet-ed that task. He is still doing the same every day. He will continue to do so in the future until the Spirit of His Father, implanted by Him in all human souls, achieves its final glory.

(V111) Current Christian Concepts on the Death and Resurrection of Christ

I attended a church service a few years ago at St. Paul's Church in my hometown of Oba, Anambra State, Nigeria. The service last-ed about two hours. The name of Jesus Christ was mentioned so many times that I lost count. All the hymns strikingly exalted Jesus. Any mention of Jesus's name was followed with a jubilant and joy-ous response that made all the people stand up and end it with "Amen". It was a performance of what Paul told the Philippians to do: "Wherefore God also hath highly exalted him, and given him a name which is above every name: That at the name of Jesus every knee should bow, of things in heaven, and things in earth, and things under the earth. (Philippians 2:9-10) Not once was the name of the Father of Jesus Christ or the God of Moses mentioned during the entire service. At the end of the service, as we were walking to the parking lot, I told a group of women what I noticed. One of them quickly replied: Jesus is our Savior.

I asked "How did He save us?

Another lady interjected: Jesus sacrificed Himself and died for us. He died for our sins.

The Christian leaders of today and the theologians, borrowed the Jewish doctrine of atonement, popularized the notion that by humans sins, inherited and acquired, God would not forgive our sins without sacrifice and that Jesus came to the world to sacrifice Himself, atone for our sins, redeem us and restore our favor with God. By His death and the blood that was shed at Golgotha, all mankind are saved! They piped this Christian faith so loud that all Christians danced with jubilation in the proclaiming that Christ died for the following reasons:

For our sins.1 Corinthians 15:3

As an act of redemption and propitiation. Romans 3:24-26

To reconciled us to God. Romans 5-10. 2 Corinthians 5:14; 6:2

As an atonement. Romans 4:24-26

To bring us to God. 1 Peter 3:18

To absorb the wrath of God. Romans 6:23. 1 John 4:10

As a ransom for many. John 3:16

Many of the above misconceptions on the death of Christ originated from the prophetic proclamations of Isaiah.

Who hath believed our report? And to whom is the arm of the LORD revealed? For he shall grow up before him as a tender plant, and as a root out of a dry ground: he hath neither form nor comeliness; and when we shall see him, there is no beauty that we should desire him. He is despised and rejected of men; a man of sorrows, and acquainted with grief: and we hid as it were our faces from him; he was despised, and we esteemed him not. Surely he hath borne our griefs, and carried our sorrows: yet we did esteem him stricken, smitten of God, and afflicted. But he was wounded for our transgressions; he was bruised for our iniquities: the chastisement of our peace was upon him; and with his stripes we are healed. All we like sheep have gone astray; we have turned everyone to his own way; and the LORD hath laid on him the iniquity of us all. He was oppressed, and he was afflicted, yet he opened not his mouth: he is brought as a lamb to the slaughter, and as a sheep before her shearers is dumb, so he opened not his mouth. He was taken from prison and from judgment: and who shall declare his generation? For he was cut off out of the land of the living: for the transgression of my people was he stricken. And he made his grave with the wicked and with the rich in his death; because he had done no violence, neither was any deceit in his mouth. Yet it pleased the LORD to bruise him; he hath put him to grief: when thou shall make his soul an offering for sin, he shall see his seed, he shall prolong his days, and the pleasure of the LORD shall prosper in his hand.

—Isaiah 53:1-10

If we are to believe in Isaiah' report then the testimony of Jesus to His apostles that "many prophets and righteous men have desired to see those things which ye see, and have not seen them; and to hear those things which ye hear, and have not heard them." (Matthew 13:17, Luke 10:24) would be meaningless. The truth as revealed by Christ is that no one, including all the Jewish prophets, had any information about His Father or Himself before He was sent to this world. The proclamation of the Prophet Isaiah completely misdirected mankind to trajectory that led to many of the misinterpretations on the death of Christ.

The ransom utterances attributed to Jesus are closely related to Isaiah report.

For even the Son of man came not to be ministered unto, but to minister, and to give his life a ransom for many.

—Mark 10:45

And he (Jesus) said unto them, this is my blood of the New Testament, which is shed for many.

—Mark 14:24

For this is my blood of the new testament, which is shed for many for the remission of sins.

—Matthew 26:28

What I found in the true Gospel of Christ are many 'weeds' that were planted in it as was portrayed in the parable of Tares. (Matthew 13:24-30) Many are accustomed to putting words in Jesus's mouth. This practice flatters when connected to Old Testament literature in the attempt to bring to light, the meaning of Jesus's words and works. The ransom sayings of Jesus are such an example, that I consider as over grown weeds choking what Jesus accomplished and demonstrated at Golgotha. Ever since those two utterances were incorporated and sown to the new clothes of the Christianity of Christ, the interpretation of the events at Golgotha became difficult. The shedding of blood for remission of sins is rooted in the Jewish belief of atonement. It is unlikely that Jesus stepped out of the box to wrap himself with the Jewish concept of salvation and sacrifice for atonement.

The promulgation and proclamation for centuries that God needs a sacrifice before He can forgive sins and that by the death of Christ, sins are forgiven, before mankind can be reconciled to God, are no longer acceptable. Jesus Christ was able to forgive sins to many people-even those that crucified Him-before His death. To promote the doctrine of redemption by the blood of Jesus, human beings were first reduced to hopeless, sinful creatures. Then the Christian leaders and the theologians took us to Golgotha and presented us with the imagery of Jesus hanging on the cross and convinced us that He suffered and was dying to save us from our sins. Thus, by His blood we are cleansed from our sins. Golgotha became the place where the Devil, who corrupted mankind with sin, was defeated. Who is to be blamed for the lack of knowledge on the significance of the death of Christ? The time has come and now is when we need knowledge about His death. Christians will have to look again at Jesus's Kingdom of God, find out what Jesus did with our gift from His Father and what He was demonstrating at Golgotha. Then follow the blood trail from Golgotha to the tomb where Jesus was buried and beyond, all the way to the day of Pentecost as to get to the right information on the death of Christ.

A good investigator knows that the blood trail from the scene of murder is most important in the attempt to identify who was responsible and why the victim was killed. To know why Jesus died, we have to follow the blood trail from the nail punctures of the hands and feet and from the stab wound on his right side, to His tomb, and then wait. Unfortunately the Christians took all the blood, disrupting the blood trail, and washed off all their sins and walked away. Then they looked at the face of God and to the Jews and found He was no longer angered at mankind. Those that followed the blood trail to the tomb and waited for forty hours witnessed the greatest miracle of all time: the resurrection of Christ! Today we celebrate Easter without knowing-as I have revealed in this treatise-the true meaning of Easter. Jesus died as part of the method He used to recreate Himself. The recreation was made manifest on Easter. In essence, Jesus was demonstrating how Himself and

His Father are creating mankind, through death and by what was showcased on Easter: the prototype of the created spiritual mankind. Those who wanted to know everything about the death and crucifixion of Jesus stayed in Jerusalem. Perhaps the news leaked out that Jesus instructed the apostles not to leave Jerusalem and to wait for the promise from His Father.

How is it we did not know this truth why Jesus died? Who disseminated the wrong information to the people after the crucible period of Christianity? Who went to all nations and proclaimed the death of Christ as an act of atonement? How can we know the truth when since it happened we were told we are miserable sinners and that the death of Christ cleansed us from our sins? Paul spoke like a Jew when he referred to the death of Jesus as "redemption through His blood, even forgiveness of sins." (Colossians 1:4)

How can we understand it when we were told that the resurrection of Jesus made Him Christ? These misunderstandings contributed immensely to why people of other religions do not agree with our Christian faith and are spiritually suspicious of Christians and the God we worship. There is no proclamation throughout the Gospel as handed down to us that is more flagrantly false than this doctrine of atoning death and the proclamation that the voluntary death of Jesus points to the elimination and forgiveness of sins. Yet they form the main pillars of today's Christianity. Who scattered the sheepfold and sent it astray to the direction of the Dead Sea? Who are the thief and the robber that "entered not by the door into the sheepfold but climbed some other way"? (John 10: 2-5)

Jesus presented to us a God that He called His Father, who is merciful and loves us. There was no word from Him that His Father is angry at humanity and out to punish us for offences we commit. He encouraged us to pray to the Father for forgiveness and prescribed that we, too, must forgive others. Those who cannot reconcile the belief that the Father of Jesus sent Him to this world to bridge the abyss of sin that separates us from Him, are at liberty to simply look elsewhere. I am one of them who decided to look elsewhere. In doing so, I took the Gospel of Christ along with me. I looked at His kingdom that came. I followed the good Shepherd of the sheep, "who gave His life for the sheep." That Jesus gave His life for the Sheep does not mean that His death was a human sacrifice to His Father. Those who followed Jesus to Golgotha became witnesses to the miracle of life as was demonstrated by Him with the Spirit of His Father in Him. We have to look at the good Shepherd on the cross that gave His life for the sheep that we may with confidence understand His demonstration of the miracle of life and benefit from that experience. This miracle of life, as I have revealed in this treatise concentrated on how Jesus is recreating Himself by His death and resurrection. It was a demonstration of the power of His Kingdom of God, Jesus's death and resurrection were the platforms He used in the execution of His miracle of life. It was an event that revealed Him, His Father and His role in human creation. His death has nothing to do with atonement, redemption, or forgiveness of sins.

"Eli, Eli lama sabachthani?"

—Jesus

The inability to comprehend what Jesus demonstrated at Golgotha has led to many esoteric assertions and demands. Even today, our inability to comprehend the spiritual demonstrations by Jesus of Nazareth at Golgotha has led to many unproven slogans of the crucifixion and death of Jesus. The misinterpretation of the Jesus's utterance, *"Eli, Eli lama sabachthani?"* as "My God, my God, why hast thou forsaken me?" is one such example. It was reported in the Gospel that "some of them that stood there when they heard that said this man calleth for Elias." That utterance was not in Aramaic, Hebrew, Greek, or any language ever known to the human race. The witness did not understand what Jesus said. The interpreters of the Gospel reviewed the Psalms of David and found what they thought was Jesus's utterance in Psalm 22:1 as "My God, my God, why hast thou forsaken me?" Jesus knew that the Father would never forsake Him. Jesus was conscious of God at all times. His inability to function outside the Father's influence placed Him on an infinite filial relationship with God that prompted Him to say, "I and the Father are one." He did not say He was God; He always called God His Father and continued to do so to the very end at Golgotha and even after His resurrection.

When the reason why Jesus died is completely dissected out and explored, what again is revealed and demonstrated by Jesus, using Himself as an example, is the journey of the human soul to its glorious destiny that would be not by the atoning death of Christ but was achieved with the infinite power Jesus's Kingdom of God. Our responsibility is this:

To be aware of "the thief that cometh not, but to steal, and to kill and destroy" and "the hired bands that cared nothing for the sheep" (John 10:2-12) The entire history of Christianity is filled up with many who came to destroy Jesus's Kingdom of God and many hired bands who cared only for themselves and what they can get, using the power and authority invested on them by the Christian communities.

Prepare our hearts as fertile grounds for growth in Jesus's Kingdom of God that we may have life and have it abundantly.

The power of the glorified Spirit of the risen Christ that was made manifest on the day of Pentecost will continue to unleash its spiritual force to attain all its goals. Along the way, every plant that His "Father did not plant will be rooted out" as it continues to strike like lightning and as thunder at the obstacles. Many temples will be destroyed. All mankind will finally turn around and worship God, our Father, in spirit and in truth.

CHAPTER 8

DECODING THE FUTURE OF
CHRISTIANITY AND MANKIND

What is really important today, as it was in the past and will be in future is this: what is the meaning of human life and where are we going? To look at the physical human body as the showcase and most important vehicle in our lives demonstrates our profound ignorance of human life and the futility of our existence. The new knowledge revealed by Jesus Christ-as I have been presenting in this treatise-compels us to look at those questions of what is happening to human life now and what will happen to it in future? No human knows the absolute truth to those questions. However, what is revealed by the words and the works of Christ exemplified by His lifestyle and demonstrated by His epic miracle of the earthly stages of the human creation, would help in guiding us to the truth. Jesus presented in the most ubiquitous demonstration and proclamations, a unified invisible power that is linked to all present human life, with its trajectory directed to the future of all mankind.

What Jesus accomplished was a showcase that revealed for the first time in the history of mankind, a spirit that appeared to many people, talked to them, allowed them to touch that spirit, and ate with humans. Such an event never happened before and probably will not happen again. If such an event occurred before, it has never been historically recorded. On his way to Damascus, Paul saw the light from that Spirit and heard His voice. The human participation in the staged evolutionary creative process, to spiritual new creatures was demonstrated by Jesus Christ. That was the vital information designed to guide us in this earthly life as we move forward in our life journey to the multiple spiritual Kingdoms in the invisible Universe.

Our lives did not begin when we were born and will not end when we die. The future will not wait for us to change. Why wait to die before you take action? Why wait to die before inheriting eternal life? Jesus did not wait for us to die before coming to meet with us. Let us rethink the way we look at our spirituality and religions or face the consequences of inaction. Do you not care about what is happening now in the world? For those that have children, do you not care about the type of world you are leaving behind? The danger to what God, the Father and Jesus Christ are creating and to the Earth environment is mankind. If we continue to resurrect major religious wars again as we did in the past and doing so now, then wild beasts, which have no religion, are better than human beings. Earthly human life is not an illusion or an entity that is speculative. What I have been presenting in this treatise that I recovered from the words and works of Christ is that human life has intrinsic value and is real; and that the spiritual world is real.

Science demands proof. It delights in scientific predictions. However, it cannot tell us about life after death and the nature of the spiritual body of the resurrected Jesus Christ. Our ability to predict the future is limited because of our lack of knowledge about who we are, why we are here, and what is contained within the spiritual worlds. Here we are, thinking that we are important, boasting of our advances in science and technology, not knowing that outside this planet, in the spiritual worlds, and perhaps even within this planet Earth, are groups of spiritual beings whose knowledge dwarfs what you see in this world today as advances in science and technology. Perhaps, what is out there in the spiritual worlds may be so large that our presence does not change anything. That the Father and Christ are creating us to come and enjoy forever, what is out there in their spiritual world, perhaps, made up of multiple Kingdoms. The Big Bang Theory and Darwin's Theory of Evolution are theories put forth to describe, at least in part, the origin of human beings. An analysis of these theories within the context of Christianity is outside the scope of what I wanted to present here. My aim is to discuss our ongoing spiritual creation starting from the onset of our reproductive cycle of humans, as we understand ourselves today.

On the other hand, it could be that a large portion of spiritual beings out there in the invisible spiritual Universe originated from this planet. A deeper reflection of Jesus's everlasting miracle of the earthly stages of human creation and His words showed that it was a demonstration of what Himself and His Father have been doing from the beginning of the reproductive phase of human creation. It is reasonable to assume that they initiated and control the origin of human species, the environment we live in and the spiritual worlds. I have in the entire epistemology of this book discussed what I have recovered from the Gospel that would help us have a glimpse into the future of mankind as prescribed, proclaimed and demonstrated by Christ. This future belongs to all of us—the entirety of humankind—together as one fold. Jesus showed by His words that we do not stand isolated from the rest of other humans on this planet. That any gift from His Father to any human being is equally given to others regardless of ethnicity, culture, nationality, or religious orientation. We are all children of God, our Father, who makes the sun to shine on the evil and on the good, and sends the rain on the just and on the unjust. [Matthew 5:44-45].

The day may come, when the truth as I have revealed in this entire treatise and what I have proclaimed as solutions to the problems facing mankind, would be seen as the truth. The need for solutions is of paramount importance. It is a concern for everyone—Jews, Christians, Muslims, Buddhists and others—that is on this Earth. It is a concern for the generations to come. The truth that I have revealed is not targeted against any religious group. When the cobwebs that have enveloped many religions as prescribed, proclaimed and practiced today are removed, what are revealed are the true Christianity of Christ and its foundational element: Jesus's Kingdom of God. When the same external components of all other world religions are removed, again what would be left is the story of the journey of the human soul and the Spirit of the true Creator God, to its ultimate end, having passed through death and resurrection, mimicking, in essence, Jesus's authentic demonstration of the earthly phase of the human creation.

I am confident that mankind will finally turn around and see the truth of Jesus's words and works. We can go on being hateful towards one another. We can continue to accumulate all the earthly treasures that will only be lost at the end of our earthly life. We can continue putting forth our prejudices, our racist and sexist attitudes. We can go on destroying properties. We can go on getting ready for wars. But to what end? I hope to live to see the day when a woman would be the Catholic Pope or the Archbishop of Canterbury. That would be the day of my 'Rapture.' That would not be an impossible event. Today as I was writing this epiphany, for the first time-a period of almost one thousand years-since the Eastern Orthodox Church and the Roman Catholic Church separated, Patriarch Krill, the head of the Russian Orthodox Church met in Cuba with Pope Frances, the head of the Roman Catholic Church. The two leaders called for unity. I am confident, that one day, with the adaptation of only what Christ, prescribed, proclaimed, manifested and demonstrated, the two groups and all Christian groups will became one entity. It took two thousand years to disrupt what was assembled by Christ. It would take another one thousand years or more to put them back again. The good news is that the solid foundation-Jesus kingdom of God-is still alive and will continue to power the human soul and fulfill all its goals for mankind.

We can continue to kill each other and glorify war as *modus operandi* of protecting our nations and liberty as we have done in the past. What we have refused to acknowledge is that the most potent weapons of mass destruction-the nuclear bombs and war heads-are imbedded and hidden in our lands and not in enemy territories. It is the same for the destructive chemical and biologic materials we plan to use against the enemy. Must we continue to develop weapons of mass destruction or create nuclear, chemical and biological arsenals for the purpose of ensuring what we presume to be our own survival? We have just recently resurrected the 'cold war.' We as Christians, pretend we do not know what is happening in Syria, Iraqi, Afghanistan, Yemen, South Sudan and other troubled places in this world we strive to makes disciples for Christ. What hypocrisy!

Must we go on preaching the diluted and corrupt 'Christian' teachings to the masses and waiting for Christ—whose Spirit came back as the Holy Spirit and is still here—to come back again as the Messiah? Must we continue to treat our Palestinian brothers and sisters as the enemy? Must we continue putting Afro-American youth behind bars, resurrecting the hate and mass incarceration of the past. That was what the author Michelle Alexander called in her book: *The New Jim Crow*. I call it resurrection of the 18th Cape Coast Castles with many doors of 'No Return' to the social and the political activities or the social benefits offered by that nation. We can re-envision a different world. We can work towards unity despite the difference in our religious beliefs, nation of birth, or skin color. The challenge as we move forward is to abandon hatred, the human tradition and doctrines we have introduced and embrace our future with Christ and reintroduce what He prescribed pro-claimed and demonstrated. Every human being is born with a purpose. We must give every human being a chance to be a par-ticipant in that glorious evolutionary process. It is what God, our Father wills and what He does. It is what He wants from us. That is the meaning of the passage: "If you love them which love you, what reward have you? Do not even the publicans do the same?" (Jesus. Matthew 5:46) Our inability to take action will not stop the evolutionary progress of the human soul because its power-Jesus's Kingdom of God-is rooted in human creation.

Heaven and earth may pass away, but my words [and my works] *will not pass away*."

—Jesus

We have wars raging across various regions of our planet. We have the migration and rising death tolls of refugees forced to flee from their homes as a result of these conflicts. We have the insatiable desire for earthy treasures. These are issues, perpetuated by peo-ple who lack understanding of what is going on, although they think they have wisdom and understanding. What is going on, but relegated to the background is the manifestation of that unifying force that would bind all humans as one fold under one God for one purpose. What is going on is the journey of the human soul through the earthly phase of spiritualization, death, and resurrec-tion under the directive of Jesus, who was given all authority and power on earth and in heaven. Unfortunately, mankind is igno-rant of that divine power. What is going on also is the gathering of all souls from the Kingdom of the dead and other spiritual worlds under the same terms as prescribed by Christ for presentation to His Father. What is going on is creation of not only humankind, but also of other living beings. Even what humans consider to be "inert" objects are undergoing their own evolutionary changes at a pace that may take millions of years for us to notice. Have you not wondered when we continue to see new stars and planets? They, too, are being created.

When and where that journey of human souls started is unknown. Jesus did not reveal it. All theories of the origin of human species are speculative. I am confident that, in the future, humans will know who we are and why we are here so as to understand the earthly phase of the journey of the human soul to its full expression. Mankind made that earthly phase the most vulnerable and dangerous stage. Man's inhumanity toward his fellow man, the unabated hatred, the proclamation of human doctrines and dogmas that divide mankind instead of unifying it, all made mankind fearful and suspicious of one another instead of inspiring people to love each other. The future belongs to all of us-the entire human race-as one fold. The question is not if it will happen, but when it happens, what trauma humans will sustain during the transitional period before it happens. The future is bright for all mankind, why destroy it for everyone?

If you are not a Christian, you would probably think that what I have presented in this book belongs to Christian concatenation and dialogue. What I have presented is the story of the earthly phase of human life. It is the story of the journey of the human soul that was made manifest by the journey of the soul of Jesus with the Spirit of His Father to its glorious end. It gave the concrete evidence of the existence of His Father, our God and the divine nature of Jesus Christ. It is the story that reveals the creative power of Jesus Christ and His Father. It is the story that reveals who we are, the intrinsic divinity in all humans, why we are here in this world and where we are going. It is a subject, whether one is spiritually dead or alive, that belongs to everyone on this planet. This is not a drill. My intention is to wake up spiritually and encourage you to participate in completing your own creation. This is the most important thing you will ever do for yourself. What you put in there is what you get. If you put nothing in, you will end up like a dead fish as Jesus revealed in the parable of Net. (Matthew 13:47-50)

I am confident that all mankind, the Jews, Christians, Muslims, Buddhists and others, will finally turn around and see the common glorious destiny of the united mankind. Nobody knows when it will happen. Will Christianity or any other world religion as prescribed, proclaimed and practiced today, claim victory for such an event? The answer is no. Along the way, it will disappear and be replaced by what I call today the new Christianity of Christ. However, Christianity of Christ may not be the name that will finally evolve in the end as name for the replacement spiritual entity. Jesus did not give a name to what He introduced to the world. When the time is fulfilled, the new name will be revealed by Jesus Christ and His Father. Whatever will evolve will bear the flagship of Jesus's kingdom of God and the stamp of His Father. There will be perpetual daily celebration in memory of Jesus's grand demonstration of the earthly journey of the human soul that allowed us to gain knowledge of our earthly and post-earthly life. Why wait to celebrate the good news? At the Last Supper, Jesus, confident that He would accomplish all His goals, instructed the apostles to celebrate and rejoice with wine and bread in His memory. He would do it again with them and all who would in the end acquire divine nature. "But I say unto you, I will not drink henceforth of this fruit of the vine, until that day when I drink it new with you in my Father's Kingdom." (Matthew 26: 29) There were no directives in it to exclude people who are not Christians or Christians who belong to another faith. It was an instruction for us to celebrate, rejoice and be happy for the victory He won for us. Christ knew what the future holds for all mankind. He was sent down by His Father to guide us to be partakers in the creation of our divine nature as to be fully created spiritual human beings and be participants in all activities in the spiritual worlds of His Father and perhaps see His glory! This is what the future holds for all mankind if we are willing to enter into His Kingdom of God enjoy all blessings and glory of that kingdom. The best of Christ is yet to come.

These things I have spoken unto you, that in me ye might have peace. In the world ye shall have tribulation: but be of good cheer; I have overcome the world.

—John 16:33

BIBLIOGRAPHY

Adams, Marilyn M. *Horrendous Evils and the Goodness of God*. Ithaca: Cornell UP, 1999.

Armstrong Karen. *A History of God*. Ballantine Book. NY. USA 1993

Anderson, Hugh, ed. *Jesus*. Englewood Cliffs: Prentice-Hall, Inc., 1967.

Aulen, Gustaf. *Dag Hammarskjold's White Book*. Philadelphia: Fortress Press, 1969.

Barclay, William. *Jesus as They Saw Him*. Grand Rapids: William B. Eerdmans Company, 1962.

Beasley Murray. *Jesus and the Kingdom of God*. The Paternoster Press. UK 1986

Bornkamm, Günther. *Jesus of Nazareth*. Trans. Irene McLuskey and Fraser McLuskey. Minneapolis: Fortress P, 1995.

. *Jesus the Human life of God*. Forward Movt. Publication. Ohio. USA. 1987

Borsch Fredrick. *God's Parable*. The Westminister Press Philadelphia. USA 1975

Bright John. *The Kingdom of God*. Abingdon Press. USA 1953

Brown, Raymond E. *The Death of the Messiah*. Vol. 2. New York: Doubleday, 1994.

Burton, Trochmorton Jr. *Gospel Parallels*. Nashville: Thomas Nelson Publishers, 1979.

Candlish James. *The Kingdom of God Biblically and Historically considered*. HardPress Publishers. Miami, Fl. USA. 1882

Carus, Paul. *The Gospel of Buddha*. Chicago: Carus Company, 2004.

Cooper, Terry D. *Dimensions of Evil*. Minneapolis: Fortress P, 2007.

Davies, Oliver, trans. *Eckhart: Selected Writings*. London: Penguin Books, 1994.1961

Davis Stephen et al *The Resurrection* Oxford University Press. USA 1997

Dodd C. H. *The Parables of the Kingdom*. Charles Scribner;s & Sons. USA

Donahue John. *The Gospel in Parables*. Fortress Press. USA 1990

Dych William. *Thy Kingdom come*. Herder and Herder Books. USA 1999

Emerson, Harry Fosdick. *The Man from Nazareth*. New York: Harper and Brothers, 1949.

Enumah, Festus. MD. *The Innocent Blood and Judas Iscariot*. Guardian Books: Canada, 2002.

Enumah Festus MD. *The Father's Business and the Spiritual Cross*. Published in Charleston.USA 2014

Fallows, Samuel Rt. Rev. *Bible Encyclopedia and Scriptural Dictionary*. Chicago: The Howard-Severance Company, 1907.

Ferguson Sinclair. *The Holy Spirit*. InterVasity Press. ILL. USA. 1996

Fite Warner. *Jesus the Man*. Harvard University Press. USA. 1946

Forde, Gerhard. *On Being a Theologian of the Cross*. Grand Rapids: William B. Eerdmans Comp., 1997.

Fosdick Harry. *The Man from Nazareth*. Harper and Brothers. NY. USA 1949

Fuellenbach John. *The Kingdom of God*. Orbis Books. NY. 1995

Goguel, Maurice. *Jesus and the Origin of Christianity*. Vols. 1 & 2. New York: Harper Torchbooks, 1960.

Gordon, D. Kaufman. *In Face of Mystery*. Cambridge: Harvard University Press, 1995.

Gordon Kaufman *Jesus and Creativity*. Fortress Press. USA 2006

Gunton C. E. *Christ and Creation*. William Eerdmans Publishing, USA 1992

Häring, Bernard. *The Law of Christ*. Trans. Edwin G. Kaiser. Westminster: The Newman P, 1963.

Harnack, Adolf. *What is Christianity?* New York: Harper & Brothers Publishers, 1957.

Harnack Adolf. *Marcion and the Gospel of Alien God*. Wipf and Stock Publishers. USA 2007

Hengel, Martin. *Crucifixion*. Philadelphia: Fortress P, 1977.

Hick, John. *Death and Eternal Life*. Louisville: Westminster/John Knox P, 1994.

Hick John *Evil and the God of Love*. Palgrave Macmillian Press USA 1977

Hoenig, Sidney B. *The Great Sanhedrin*. Philadelphia: Bloch Publishing Co. 1953.

Holland Henry Scott. *God's City and the coming of the Kingdom*. Longmans, Green & Co NY. USA 1987

The Holy Bible, Original King James Version. Gordonsville: Dugan Publishers Inc., 1985.

Jackson Samuel Macauley. *The new Schaff-Herzog Encyclopedia of Religious Knowledge*.

Baker Book House. Grand Rapid. Michigan. USA 1950

Jeremias Joachin *Jerusalem in Times of Jesus*. Philadelphia: Fortress Press, 1969.

Jeremias, Joachim..*The Parables of Jesus*. Prentice-Hall. USA 1963

Kaufman Gordon *God the Problem*. Harvard University Press. USA. 1972

Kaufmann Walter (Introducer) *Religion from Tolstoy to Camus*. Harper Torch Books. N.Y. 1961

Kim Kirsteen. *The Holy Spirit in the world*. Orbis Books. NY. USA 2007

Kittay, Eva F. *Metaphor*. Oxford: Clarendon P, 1989

Ladd George. *The Gospel of the Kingdom*. William B. Eerdmans Publishers. USA

Lakoff, George, and Mark Johnson. *Metaphors We Live By*. Chicago: University of Chicago P, 1980.

Linwood Urban *A short history of Christian thoughts*. Oxford University Press 1995.

Lockyer, Herbert. *All the Messiah Prophecies of the Bible*. Grand Rapids: Zondervan Publishing House, 1960.

McConkie Jeseph et al. *The Holy Spirit*. Bookcraft. Utah. USA 1989

Mclnerny, D. Q. *Being Logical*. New York: Random House, 2004.

Meeks, Wayne A., ed. *The Writings of St. Paul*. New York: W. W. Norton & Company, Inc., 1972.

Moltmann Jurgen. *God in Creation*. Fortress Press. Minneapolis. USA 1993

Nelson-Pallmeyer. *Jesus against Christianity*. Harrisburg, Penn.: Trinity Press International, 2001.

Norman Beck. *Mature Christianity in the 21ˢᵗ Century*. Crossroad. NY, USA 1994

O'Malley Williams. *God the oldest Question*. Loyola Press. ILL. USA 2000

Pelikan, Jaroslav. *Jesus Through the Centuries*. New York: Harper & Row, 1985.

Pink Arthur. *The Beatitudes and the Lord's Prayer*. Baker Books. USA 1979

Richards, Lawrence O. *The Word Bible Handbook*. Waco: Word, Inc., 1982.

Sanday, William. *The International Critical Commentary on the Holy Scripture of the Old and New Testaments*. New York: Charles Scribners Sons, 1920.

Schillebeeckx, Edward. *Jesus: An experiment in Christology*. New York: Seabury, 1979.

Sheen, Fulton J. *Life of Christ*. New York: Image Books Doubleday. 1958.

Schweitzer Albert *The mystery of the Kingdom of God*. Dodd, Mead Publishers. USA 1914

Simkhovitch, Vladimir. *Toward the Understanding of Jesus.* New York: The MacMillan Company,1925.

Spong John Shelby. *Liberating the Gospels.* HarperSan Francisco. USA 1996

Stott, John. *The Cross of Christ.* Downers Grove: InterVarsity P, 1986.

Thompson Marianne Meye. *The Promise of the Father.* Westminister John Knox Press. USA. 2000

Tolstoy Leo. *The Kingdom of God is within you.* University of Nebraska Press USA. 1984

Townshend, George. *The Heart of the Gospel.* London: Templar Printing Works, 1939.

Toynbee, Arnold. *The Crucible of Christianity.* New York: The World Publishing Company, 1969.

Wesley John. *The nature of the Kingdom.* Bethany House Publishers. USA. 1979.

Wilson, Ian. *Jesus: The Evidence.* New York: Harper Collins Publishers, 1984.

Wood, et al. *Immanuel Kant: Religion within the Boundaries of Mere Reason And Other Writings.* Cambridge: Cambridge UP, 1998.

Dr. Festus Enumah will arrange a part of his share of the proceeds from this book to be donated International Refugee Organizations and other Organization who are relentlessly working to control the conditions that create the refugee problems

ABOUT THE AUTHOR

Dr. Festus Enumah graduated from the University of Ibadan Medical School and Government College while living in Nigeria. He went on to train at Cook County Hospital in Chicago and at the University of Texas M. D. Anderson Cancer Center in Houston and is a board-certified surgeon with years of experience. Dr. Enumah is the founder and president of the Samuel A. Enumah Africancer Foundation, a US nonprofit that plans to build sustainable cancer detection and treatment in sub-Saharan Africa.

Over the years, Dr. Enumah has also penned *The Innocent Blood and Judas Iscariot* and *The Father's Business and the Spiritual Cross.*

When he's not working, researching, or writing books, Dr. Enumah enjoys spending time with his wife, Lois, and their four children. He also relishes having time to play golf and tennis, and he collects Bibles and rare books on Christianity.

www.ingramcontent.com/pod-product-compliance
Lightning Source LLC
Chambersburg PA
CBHW032005040426
42448CB00006B/488